Natural
Wonders
— *of* —
New York

Natural
Wonders
of
New York

A Guide to
Parks, Preserves
& Wild Places

Deborah Williams

Illustrated by Lois Leonard Stock

Country Roads Press

CASTINE · MAINE

Natural Wonders of New York:
A Guide to Parks, Preserves & Wild Places
© 1995 by Deborah Williams. All rights reserved.

Published by Country Roads Press
P.O. Box 286, Lower Main Street
Castine, Maine 04421

Text and cover design by Studio 3, Ellsworth, Maine.
Cover photograph courtesy of New York State Department
    of Economic Development.
Illustrations by Lois Leonard Stock.
Typesetting by Typeworks, Belfast, Maine.

ISBN 1-56626-080-9

Library of Congress Cataloging-in-Publication Data

Williams, Deborah.
    Natural wonders of New York : a guide to parks, preserves and
wild places / author, Deborah Williams ; illustrator, Lois Leonard
Stock.
        p.   cm.
    Includes index.
    ISBN 1-56626-080-9 : $9.95
    1. New York (State) – Guidebooks.   2. Natural history – New
York (State) – Guidebooks.   3. Natural areas – New York (State) –
Guidebooks.   4. Parks – New York (State) – Guidebooks.
    5. Botanical gardens – New York (State) – Guidebooks.   I. Title.
    F117.3.W553   1995
    917.4704′43 – dc20   94-37144
                                                                                              CIP

Printed in the United States of America.
10   9   8   7   6   5   4   3   2   1

*To Thomas Rees Williams II,
who taught me a love of the woods,
water, and words*

It is an incalculable added pleasure to anyone's sum of happiness if he or she grows to know, even slightly and imperfectly, how to read and enjoy the wonder book of nature.

— Theodore Roosevelt

Contents

Introduction

Whatever befalls the earth,
befalls the sons and daughters of the earth.
—Chief Seattle

For years I rushed through the Montezuma Wildlife Refuge as I drove sixty mph along the New York Thruway. Occasionally I saw flocks of geese flying overhead, but I was always too busy to stop and actually visit the refuge. When I finally did stop, I saw bald eagles on a nest, ducks aplenty, and flocks of geese. Park rangers were on hand to answer questions and give advice on where to see the rarer birds.

New York State is often like this—there are natural wonders galore for those who are willing to slow down, stop, and look. The state has a unique variety of natural habitats and ecosystems. From the sandy beaches and salt marshes of Long Island to the alpine lakes and high peaks of the Adirondacks, and from the valley of the mighty Hudson River to the shores of the Great Lakes, there is no place in the United States quite like New York.

Some of the state's wonders, such as Niagara Falls, are

world famous and have almost become tourist clichés. They remain awesome and worthy of a visit—Niagara Falls has the distinction of being the nation's first state park.

Lovers of nature owe much to New Yorker Theodore Roosevelt, the nation's most ardent conservationist, whose regard for the natural world undoubtedly was shaped during his summers in the wilds of the Adirondacks.

Many of New York's most sublime natural resources have been protected by farseeing philanthropists of the nineteenth and early twentieth centuries. But development, population, and pollution are encroaching upon nature and our precious natural heritage. Acid rain doesn't respect the boundaries of the Adirondacks. Ocean pollution affects the beaches of Long Island. Chemical pollution has brought state warnings against eating fish caught in the Great Lakes.

Hiking in the high peaks of the Adirondacks has become so popular that a permit system is being developed, to prevent the area's being loved to death. Everyone who uses hiking trails owes it to future generations to respect the rules that go with them.

The popularity of camping and the outdoors has meant increased interest in the state's parks. There are good and bad aspects to this attention. More use means more pressure on the parks, but we hope it also means more nature lovers and more pressure to preserve our natural heritage.

My seven-year-old niece, Heather, lives on Otisco Lake in the Finger Lakes. She has been camping and canoeing since she was an infant. She now has her own canoe paddle, cross-country skis, backpack, fishing rod, and binoculars. She recognizes scores of birds, animal tracks, the planets in the sky, and many constellations. Unlike Heather, many children have had little contact with nature. All of us must help to expose more children to their heritage and preserve the glory of New York's natural world for Heather's children and grandchildren.

The Roger Tory Peterson Institute of Natural History in Jamestown is dedicated to creating passion and concern for the natural world in the hearts and minds of children, the future stewards of the earth. Every one of us owes it to our world to work to create that love of nature among children.

Every day, children are enjoying Tifft Nature Preserve, a unique urban wildlife preserve in Buffalo built on a garbage dump. Birds, mammals, fish, and flowers are at home in this preserve in the shadow of former steel mills. If nature can flourish here, it can flourish just about anywhere—with some help.

ETHICS AND SAFETY

Common sense and concern for nature and others will help ensure that your visits to parks and the wilderness are safe. They will also help to preserve natural places for others.

• **Wildlife and plant life:** Do not deface, remove, or injure trees, plants, fossils, or minerals found on public lands. It is very harmful to drive nails into trees or peel their bark.

• **Litter and sanitation:** Dispose of garbage, sewage, and wastewater in proper receptacles. On the trail, carry out what you carry in. For human wastes, dig a shallow hole at least 150 feet from any water or trail. Bury your wastes and cover them with leaf litter and dirt. Do not wash in the lakes and streams.

• **Fires:** At the campgrounds, build fires only in designated fireplaces. On the trail, build fires only when necessary. Never leave any fire unattended. Wood on state lands can be burned only if the wood is already dead and down.

• **Wild animals:** Rabies has reached epidemic levels in most parts of the state. Any mammal can contract rabies. Do not touch or feed any wild animal. Immediately contact the park police if you are bitten by a wild animal. Do not store food or garbage on the ground or in your tent; secure it in your vehicle or hang it from a rope between two trees at least fifteen feet above the ground.

 • **Noise:** Obey the rules concerning quiet hours in the park. People come to parks to escape the noise of people and civilization.

 • **Safety:** It is best not to hike alone. Be sure to sign in at the trail stations. Be prepared for changing weather, especially in the high peaks of the Adirondacks. On one October visit we made to Lake Placid, it was summer-like in the morning and snowing lightly by evening.

NEW YORK STATE INFORMATION

New York State Dept. of Economic Development
Division of Tourism
One Commerce Plaza
Albany, NY 12245
800-CALL-NYS

Caving

Northern Pathfinders
PO Box 6568
Albany, NY 12206
518-459-4966

Climbing

Alpine Adventures
PO Box 179, Route 73
Keene, NY 12942
518-576-9881

Ascents of Adventure
PO Box 6568
Albany, NY 12206
518-459-4966

Hiking

Adirondack Mountain Club
RR3, Box 3055
Lake George, NY 12845
518-668-4447

Appalachian Mountain Club
Manhattan Resource Center
202 East 39th Street
New York, NY 10016
212-986-1430

Finger Lakes
  Trail Conference
PO Box 18048
Rochester, NY 14618-0048
716-288-7191

Long Island Greenbelt
  Trail Conference
23 Deer Path Road
Central Islip, NY 11722
516-360-0753

New York–New Jersey
  Trail Conference
232 Madison Avenue
New York, NY 10016
212-685-9699

Guides

There are more than 300 professional guides who have met New York State licensing requirements. For *A Guide to the Outdoor Guides of New York State* write to:

New York Outdoor Guides Association
PO Box 916 NYS
Saranac Lake, NY 12983

More than 800 miles of trails in New York state parks accommodate hikers of all abilities and experience. For the *Guide to New York State Operated Parks, Historic Sites and Their Programs* write to:

State Parks
Albany, NY 12238

For *Use of New York State's Public Forest Lands* write to:

DEC License Sales
50 Wolf Road, Room 111
Albany, NY 12233-4790

Camping

There are more than 500 public and privately owned camp-grounds in the state.

Call 800-456-CAMP for reservations for state-run campsites and cabins. Hearing-impaired campers can use TDD 800-274-7275 or TTY 800-662-1220. Call from ninety days up to seven days before your stay.

For a list of privately owned campgrounds write:

Campground Owners of NY
PO Box 497
Dansville, NY 14437
716-335-2710
(include a $2 check or money order for postage and handling)

For *Opening the Outdoors to People with Disabilities* write:

NYS DEC
50 Wolf Road
Albany, NY 12233
518-457-2500

Want to try camping but don't have any gear? The Department of Environmental Conservation rents fully equipped campsites in the Adirondacks and Catskills. All you need is food, clothing, and personal items—experienced DEC campground personnel will even help you get settled.

Space is limited, so reservations and advance payment are required and will be accepted on a first-come, first-served basis. At Mongaup Pond campground near Livingston Manor in the Catskills, the fee is $13.00 per day. For $15.00 a day, you can stay at Fish Creek Pond near Tupper Lake in the Adirondacks. Both campgrounds also require a $1.50 registration fee. Up to six campers can use a site for a minimum of three to a maximum of seven days.

For information and reservations in the Catskills, call 914-255-5453; in the Adirondacks, call 518-897-1309.

Fishing

A license is needed by anyone 16 or older, resident or nonresident, who wants to fish New York's fresh waters. Residents 65 or older are eligible for licenses at a reduced fee of $5.00, as are veterans with forty percent or greater service-connected disability. The legally blind and certain members of Native American tribes are entitled to free licenses, with proper certification. Obtain details from the New York State Department of Environmental Conservation (DEC). Write to:

DEC
50 Wolf Road
Albany, NY 12233-4790

Fishing Hotlines

DEC Region 5
518-891-5413 (Ray Brook)
518-623-3682 (Warrensburg)

DEC Region 7
607-753-1551

Salmon River
315-298-6531 (Pulaski)

Finger Lakes
315-536-7480

Wayne County
315-946-5466

Monroe County
716-987-8800

Orleans County
716-682-4223

DEC Region 9
716-885-3474

Niagara County
716-433-5606

Hunting

Small-game licenses are required for hunters age 12 and over; big-game licenses are required for hunters 16 and older. Junior archery licenses may be purchased by 14- and 15-year-olds with certification of both hunter and bow-hunter training. All first-time hunters must complete a ten-hour hunter-safety training course, offered free by volunteer instructors. Bow hunters must also complete an archery training course before buying a New York license. Training certificates issued by other states and provinces are accepted for firearms hunting.

Licenses are available at DEC regional offices, town and county clerk offices, some state campgrounds, and many sporting-goods stores, bait shops, and similar outlets.

State Park Passes

The **Empire Passport** provides vehicle entry, for residents or nonresidents, to nearly 200 state parks and recreation areas for a full year from April 1 to March 31. Purchases can be made in person at most parks for $30 or by mail from Passport, State Parks, Albany, NY 12238.

The **Golden Park Program** provides New York State residents 62 or older free entry to state parks and recreation areas any weekday, excluding holidays, as well as reduced fees for some activities. Simply present your current New York State driver's license or Non-Driver's Identification Card.

The **Access Pass** provides New York State residents who have certain permanent disabilities free entry to most New York State parks and recreation areas and free use of many of their facilities. For an application or detailed information contact: Access, State Parks, Albany, NY 12238, or any state park.

Long Island

MONTAUK POINT STATE PARK

There's a delicious feeling of apartness at Montauk Point State Park on the eastern tip of Long Island. The last spot of land before the roaring Atlantic, and 132 miles from New York City, Montauk bills itself as "where Long Island begins."

The tip of Long Island and the park are guarded by the Montauk Point Lighthouse. Authorized by President George Washington in 1792, the 110-foot lighthouse has been part of the seascape since the eighteenth century. It is the oldest lighthouse in New York and the fourth-oldest active lighthouse in the United States.

It was on November 5, 1797, that Jacob Hand lit the wicks of thirteen whale oil lamps and a light shone from the Montauk Point Lighthouse for the first time. Hand, the first keeper of the lighthouse, stood watch all night, checking the oil supply, trimming the wicks, and cleaning the storm panes of soot.

The walls of the lighthouse are six feet thick at the base, three feet thick at the top. The light rotates every five seconds and can be seen for nineteen nautical miles. Members of the U.S. Lighthouse Service and the U.S. Coast Guard have been the resident keepers.

Whaling ships, steamers, submarines, and fishing and sailing vessels of all kinds have passed this tower on Turtle Hill, guided and reassured by its presence. Automated by the Coast Guard in 1987, the Montauk Point Lighthouse no longer needs a lightkeeper. However, under a program to provide for maintenance and preservation, the Coast Guard has leased the lighthouse to the Montauk Historical Society. The society maintains the lighthouse and the surrounding property, fighting an ongoing battle against erosion.

There are 137 iron steps to the top of the tower. On a clear day the view is breathtaking. However, you don't need to make the trek to the top to get a great view of Connecticut, Rhode Island, and Block Island.

Montauk County Park, adjacent to the state park, offers terrific vistas of Block Island Sound and Block Island. The park is home to many species of wildflowers and is visited by a variety of migrating birds.

Trails wind their way past the long-deserted village of the Montauk Indians, the area's first inhabitants, who allowed white settlers to graze their cattle on the hills that are now part of the park. In the early 1800s, a house was built on the southern edge of the park to provide shelter for cattle keepers. Known as Third House, it now contains park offices. Teddy Roosevelt stayed at Third House when he and the Rough Riders returned from the Spanish American War. Some 25,000 troops, victims of yellow fever, recuperated in Montauk.

Fishing and surfing are both popular at Montauk Point State Park. There's a restaurant at the park and gift shops at the lighthouse and in the restaurant. There are also picnic facilities. The county park has a beach, a bicycle hostel area, five miles of bridle paths with horse rentals, outer beach camping, freshwater

**Try surf casting for striped bass and bluefish,
especially if the summer is cool**

fishing on Big Reed Pond, waterfowl and deer hunting with
proper licenses, and an Indian Museum.

Where: The state and county parks are at the easternmost tip of
Long Island. From New York City take the Long Island Express-
way to exit 66 to State 27 to the end.
Hours: The parks are open throughout the year, from dawn to
dusk. The lighthouse is open for tours from 10:00 A.M. to 4:00
P.M., Memorial Day weekend through Labor Day weekend.
Admission: $3.00 per car to the state park May 28 through
Labor Day; free the rest of the year. Admission to the lighthouse
is $2.50 per adult, $1.00 for children 6–12. The county park
technically is open only to Suffolk County residents with a Green

Key Pass. Admission is tightly enforced during the busy summer season. During the rest of the year, nonresidents should have no problem visiting the park.

Best time to visit: Late spring or early fall is a good time to enjoy the warm weather and avoid crowds.

Activities: Fishing, surfing, picnicking, bicycling, horseback riding, camping, hunting, museum.

Pets: Must be on a leash. Not allowed in the lighthouse.

For more information:

Montauk Point State Park, Montauk Point, NY 11954; 516-668-2461.

Montauk Point Lighthouse, Montauk Historical Society, PO Box 942, Montauk, NY 11954; 516-668-2544.

Montauk County Park, East Lake Drive, Montauk, NY 11954; 516-852-7878.

HITHER HILLS STATE PARK

The major lure of Hither Hills State Park is the camping it offers along a beautiful stretch of the Atlantic. The park's wide sandy beach extends for more than two miles and also attracts day visitors.

At campsites just over the dunes, you can slip off to sleep listening to the lapping or crash of the waves, depending on wind conditions. Although the sites are quite close together and there are few trees in the camping area for shade or privacy, Hither Hills presents an unparalleled opportunity to experience life on the beach. The campsites extend along the Atlantic, but the park extends the full width of Montauk to Napeague Bay in the north — 1,755 acres in all. There's a forty-acre freshwater fishing pond, a softball field, and hiking and nature trails.

Of course, saltwater fishing is a prime attraction here, and

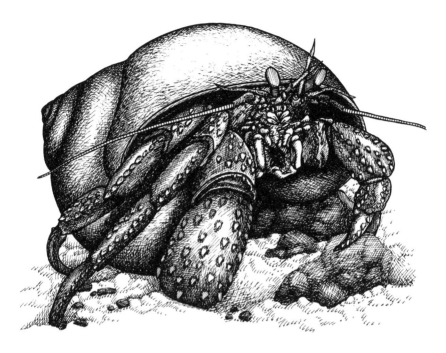

Hermit crabs are always at home—although they sometimes outgrow their homes and search for larger models

campers can be out on the beach surf casting for bluefish and striped bass before the sun rises.

Where: Hither Hills is four miles west of Montauk, off State 27 (Montauk Highway).
Hours: Daily, sunrise to sunset. Campsites are open April 30 to November 20.
Admission: $4.00 per car, May 31 to September 6.
Best time to visit: September is a wonderful time to visit, because the crowds have gone and the water is still warm.
Activities: Camping, fishing, hiking, nature walks.

Pets: Must be on a leash.
Other: There's a general store, which is open weekends only to October 25.
For more information:
    Hither Hills State Park, Montauk, NY; 516-668-2461.
    Campsites reservations, 800-456-CAMP.

FIRE ISLAND NATIONAL SEASHORE

Fire Island stretches thirty-two miles from Democrat Point on the west to Moriches Inlet on the east. This skinny, string-bean-shaped barrier island faces the Atlantic Ocean while protecting the waters of Great Sound Bay and the mainland of Long Island at its back.

People have created seventeen separate communities on Fire Island for summer living and recreation, but they have made efforts to preserve the natural life, too. Varying in width from a quarter of a mile to just a few hundred feet, the island presents a remarkable mixture of natural environments.

Fire Island exists because of sand stranded or blown beyond the reach of the tides, then captured by beach grass. The plant's Latin name is *Ammophila briviligulata,* which means "lover of sand."

Nature is everywhere here. On our first night on Fire Island we spotted a trio of deer happily munching on a summer resident's bushes. Over the dunes, a great blue heron strolled daintily along the beach.

Fire Island National Seashore, less than forty miles from New York City, consists of the unsettled and protected areas of the island between several communities.

Four separate areas make up the national seashore. Access to the Lighthouse Area in the west and the Smith Point Area in the east is by car. The two areas in the heart of the island, Watch Hill and Sailors Haven, can be reached only by water taxi or private boat, or by ferry from Long Island (in season). In between are clusters of small communities, but no roads.

The area closest to the city is the Lighthouse Visitors Center. Take the Robert Moses Causeway from West Islip to the Lighthouse Area, which borders Robert Moses State Park.

As might be expected, Fire Island has long been a land of shipwrecks. The first recorded wreck occurred on May 8, 1657. Many more wrecks over the next century or more led to the building of the lighthouse, which began operation in 1826. The current brick, striped lighthouse was completed in 1858.

It's a walk of just over a half mile to the lighthouse from the closest parking lot. The visitors center is housed in the stone building next to the lighthouse, formerly the keeper's home. Displays inside tell tales of a lonely life here before bridges made a connection to Long Island. The displays also offer a glimpse into the island's days as a haven for rumrunners during Prohibition.

Pick up a trail leaflet in the visitors center and take the half-mile boardwalk trail past sand dunes and cranberry bogs, along the shore of Great South Bay. Notice the trees with bald south sides, the result of the constant blowing of salt winds. Remember to stay on the boardwalk, not only to protect the fragile dunes and plants but also to avoid the poison ivy, which grows in abundance throughout the island, and to reduce the chances of being bitten by the ticks that cause Lyme disease.

The National Park Service offers regular interpretive walks and programs on everything from the lighthouse's history to sing-alongs of old sea chanteys.

Sailors Haven area, the next national seashore area heading east, is accessible only by boat. Most visitors arrive via a half-hour ferry ride from the mainland.

As you near Fire Island, anticipation runs high. There is

something special about visiting an island, especially on a perfect summer day. The ferry pulls in, dropping off a cheerful parade of visitors toting beach gear and picnics.

The first stop for many is the visitors center, where you can pick up a trail guide. Children head for the "touch me" table, to feel a tube worm, crab, or other sea creature. Park rangers are on hand to answer questions. Check the schedule for nature programs, including the opportunity to built a gigantic communal sand castle with the assistance of a park ranger or go seining in the bay. Guided tours of the Sunken Forest are held each afternoon during the summer.

The Sunken Forest is the jewel of Fire Island. Imagine entering an eerie woodland with gnarled branches—a forest primeval and a botanical wonderland at the same time.

The climate on the island can be harsh, as winds batter trees and stunt their growth. But here between high dunes is the Sunken Forest, a dense expanse of trees, bushes, and vines, protected from the sea winds. The trail is actually a network of well-maintained boardwalks that extend for a mile and a half through the forest.

This is a forest unlike any you have experienced. Ocean salt kills vegetation, so when the foliage reaches the height of the dunes, it begins to grow horizontally instead of vertically. Gnarled holly, sassafras, tupelo, and shadblow form a protective canopy over vines of catbrier, poison ivy, and wild grape as they climb from the forest floor toward the sun. The result is a lovely, delicate canopy that forms a dark, cool respite from the hot sun. Of the thirty-five markers identified in the trail booklet, this is marker number 19, the highlight of the walk for many.

As you follow the boardwalk, you will come upon benches where you can stop to rest and enjoy the scenery. There are even a few elevated spots that provide glimpses of ocean and bay. Many birds make their homes in the forest, and their songs provide a pleasant accompaniment for your walk. We didn't spot any deer on a recent visit, although other walkers had spotted a lone deer in the forest during the morning.

From the Sunken Forest Trail there's a trail to the beach, which offers showers, changing rooms, a snack bar and gift shop, and a thirty-six-slip marina for private boats. A lifeguard is on duty during the summer.

The next seashore area to the east is Watch Hill, the only family campground on Fire Island and accessible only by boat

Sanderlings rush up the beach ahead of a wave and then skitter back to search for crustaceans stranded by the retreating waves

or ferry. The park service recommends that campers with heavy or large amounts of equipment bring a cart or wagon to help haul their gear to the campground, which is about a quarter-mile from the ferry terminal along a boardwalk trail. Competition is intense for the twenty-six campsites, for which there is a four-night limit. Reservations are necessary, and campers are usually selected by lottery.

There's a small visitors center, a nature trail, a snack bar, showers, a 158-slip marina, and a swimming beach with a lifeguard.

Seven miles east of Watch Hill is Smith Point, the only federally designated wilderness area in New York. With the exception of a boardwalk trail for the handicapped at Smith Point West, the wilderness is accessible only by foot.

Only primitive camping is allowed in the wilderness area, and campers must be completely self-sufficient. Fall and spring are the best seasons for camping, as summer's masses of mosquitoes can be most annoying.

If you are willing to invest the time and energy, a hike in the wilderness area will reveal a view of the island as it was when the first Europeans saw it 400 years ago. Each season has its attractions. During the spring and fall, migrating waterfowl bob on the protected waters of Great South Bay. Fire Island is on the Atlantic Flyway, a major migratory route. During the winter the beaches are deserted and starkly beautiful. Of course, Fire Island seems to have been created for the special joys of summer— beaches, swimming, and fishing.

Smith Point West can be reached by car via the William Floyd Parkway and Smith Point Bridge. There's a visitors center, a nature trail, and various ranger-led walks on which you can learn about shells, shipwrecks, and edible plants growing on the island. Hunting and recreational permits are available at the visitors center. Fishing is good year-round. In Great South Bay, there's bluefish, striped bass, winter flounder. Surf casters cast their lines for striped bass, bluefish, mackerel, and weakfish. Hunting permits are available at Smith Point.

Where: To reach the Lighthouse Area from State 27, take exit 41, then take the Robert Moses Parkway south. Cross the Robert Moses Causeway and continue to the island. To reach Sailors Haven from State 27, take Lakeland Avenue south onto Main Street and follow the green and white signs for Fire Island Ferries. To reach Watch Hill from State 27, take Waverly Avenue south to the ferry terminal. To reach Smith Point West from State 27, take exit 58, then take the William Floyd Highway south and cross Smith Point Bridge to the island.

Hours: The seashore is open year-round; Sailors Haven Marina is open late April to mid-October, and Watch Hill Marina is open mid-May to mid-October. Ferries generally run early May through October.

Admission: Free, although fees are charged for the ferry ride and parking at the ferry terminals. Parking fees are charged during the summer for the beaches at Robert Moses State Park and Smith Point County Park.

Best time to visit: The peak season is late June through Labor Day weekend. September is usually warm enough for swimming, and the crowds have mostly gone. Weekends are always busier than weekdays.

Activities: Nature programs, camping, swimming, boating, hiking, bird-watching, fishing.

Pets: Must be on a leash.

For more information:

Superintendent, Fire Island National Seashore, 120 Laurel Street, Patchogue, NY 11772; 516-289-4810.

Summer camping applications are accepted in February and March for a drawing in April. For an application, write to the superintendent and enclose a self-addressed stamped envelope. However, no-shows are common, even in the summer. You can

call 516-597-6633 to check on last-minute availability. If there is
no space available and you want to put up your tent, you can
check out Heckscher State Park, just one mile from East Islip.
Call 516-581-2100.

JONES BEACH STATE PARK

Jones Beach State Park, the most famous and magnificent of all
Long Island state parks, is named after Major Thomas Jones, a
man with a colorful history.

Jones was an Irish soldier of fortune who had been a loser
in the Battle of the Boyne and the Siege of Limerick. He later
escaped to France, where he obtained a ship and crew to prey on
commerce as a privateer. This was considered a respectable
international practice, but not by the British when it affected their
shipping. They soon trapped his ship in the West Indies, where it
had to be abandoned.

Major Jones arrived on Long Island in 1692 and shortly became Sheriff of Queens County and Ranger General of Nassau.
Following his marriage to Freelove Townsend, he became owner
of one of the largest tracts of land on the South Shore. The couple
settled down on the vast acreage around Massapequa given to the
bride as a wedding gift by her father. They built the first brick
house on Long Island and eventually acquired a total of 6,000
acres. Apparently they thought they also owned at least part of
what is now Jones Beach, because around 1700 Jones established
a whaling station on the outer beach near the site of the present
park.

Separating the Atlantic Ocean from Great South Bay on
the South Shore of Long Island, the outer beach was a lonely,
windswept sand reef half a mile wide. On the ocean side were
rolling sand dunes with a sparse growth of dune vegetation.
North of the dunes, salt marshes stretched to the bay. Seldom

visited, the beach was isolated from the mainland and practically inaccessible, even by boat, because of the intricate network of grassy islands in the shallow waters of the bay.

No one knows how long the Jones whaling plant operated. For more than 200 years the outer beach, known as Jones Beach, including sections called Hemlock Beach, High Hill Beach, Short Beach, Gilgo Beach, Cedar Beach, and Oak Beach, remained virtually uninhabited and unused. A few fishermen's shacks and summer cottages were the only visible signs of human life.

In the early 1920s, conditions were described by Birdsall Jackson of Wantagh, an author and historian: "In the sailboat with a fair wind, the trip to Jones Beach took about an hour, and with a head wind, three hours. If you were not familiar with the many shoals and crooked channels you would not get there at all. An excursion to Jones Beach was always planned as a full day's outing and the day chosen so the voyager went out with the ebb tide and came back with the flood. All night sojourns on the sand flats were not infrequent."

In 1925, the Long Island State Park Commission, under the leadership of President Robert Moses, began negotiations for acquisition of the outer beach and adjacent lands. On the park's opening day — August 4, 1929 — a howling wind and sandstorm nearly brought the opening festivities to a halt and provided a field day for critics of the Jones Beach project. The completion of lawn areas and the planting of millions of clumps of beach grass prevented further sandstorms. The success and popularity of Jones Beach soon became apparent. In 1930, the first full year of operation, a million and a half people visited the park.

From the beginning, everything about Jones Beach has been grand. It was the dream of Robert Moses, a man who loved to build and create.

What can you say about a park with parking fields for 23,000 cars, a landmark water tower that holds 300,000 gallons of water, eight ocean bathing areas, 250 lifeguards, two Olympic-sized pools? The freshwater supply comes from four wells, each more than 1,000 feet deep. Five miles of ocean beach frontage and a half mile of bay frontage have been developed for swimming. There are nearly 12,000 lockers and dressing rooms in the two bathhouses, seventeen cafeterias and refreshment stands, three restaurants, and nearly two miles of boardwalk. A clean, well-maintained park, Jones Beach has something to offer just about everyone.

Fishing is popular here. A bait station and fishing piers can be used for bay fishing at Field 10. Beach areas at West End 2 and Field 6 are designated for surf fishing with proper permits.

The 8,206-seat Jones Beach Theatre opened in 1952. The concrete-and-steel structure replaced the wooden grandstand erected in the 1930s with the help of work-relief forces. The theater's premiere production was Michael Todd's *A Night in Venice*, which ran for two seasons. In 1954, Guy Lombardo took the production reins with his presentation of *Arabian Nights*. The 1954 season was the first of twenty-four seasons and fourteen different shows for Lombardo and the Royal Canadians. His nightly arrival at the helm or on the deck of his speedboat *Tempo* was as eagerly awaited as the first notes of each overture. Musical extravaganzas have continued to be produced each summer since Lombardo's death.

Where: Jones Beach is about thirty-three miles from Manhattan. Take the Southern State Parkway east to Meadowbrook or Wantagh Parkway south to Jones Beach State Park. During the summer there is train service to Freeport or Wantagh and scheduled bus service to the park; 212-739-4200. There is also bus service from mid-Manhattan; 718-788-8000.
Hours: The park is open throughout the year.
Admission: $4.00 per car from May 28 through September 5; free otherwise.
Best time to visit: Summer is the most popular time to visit, and

weekends can be very crowded. If you want to visit on a summer weekend, arrive before 9:00 A.M., if possible. Otherwise, May or September can be beautiful and relatively uncrowded, especially during the week.

Activities: Ballfields, bicycling, fishing, pitch 'n' putt golf with club rental, miniature golf, hiking and exercise trails, picnicking, freshwater and saltwater swimming, basketball courts, roller skating, bathhouses with showers and lockers, and Jones Beach Theatre.

Pets: Not allowed.

For more information:

Jones Beach State Park, Ocean Drive, Wantagh, NY 11793; 516-785-1600. For information and concert schedules for Jones Beach Theatre, 516-221-1000.

HECKSCHER STATE PARK

Heckscher State Park on Great South Bay in East Islip today is a lovely and serene place. Most park visitors would be surprised to learn of the complex legal history of these parklands.

Before the park was established, it was the subject of litigation in a variety of courts—from the County Court of Suffolk County to the Supreme Court of the United States. The case produced twenty-five separate appellate proceedings and a special summer session of the state legislature, and it held up the expenditure of park funds throughout the state for nearly a year. It was the subject of mass meetings, pamphlets, and newspaper campaigns, and it was instrumental in changing the route of a parkway more than thirty miles away.

The property involved the George C. Taylor estate of more than 1,600 acres on Great South Bay. Known as an eccentric of considerable means, Taylor assembled the tract and in 1886 built a large and ornate country home with about thirty auxiliary buildings. He stocked the wooded areas with deer and game birds and had peacocks and a herd of elk wandering about.

In the summer of 1924 the newly created Long Island State Park Commission was looking for locations for new state parks and for a headquarters for the commission's staff. Opposition arose when it became known that the state intended to acquire the Taylor property. Wealthy residents, afraid that the park would be detrimental to the neighborhood, mounted an intense campaign to block the public project.

August Heckscher, long a champion of public recreation facilities, became interested in the controversy and decided to give the state $262,000 to enable the commission to pay for the property. More legal wrangling ensued. Finally, on June 2, 1929, the controversy ended, and the park name was changed to Heckscher State Park. The park was immediately popular.

It boasts more than three miles of frontage on Great South Bay. There's a swimming pool and bathhouse on South Beach. The parkway provides a scenic drive. At dusk, herds of deer emerge from the wooded areas to feed.

Where: Off Hechscher State Parkway in East Islip, 50 miles from New York City.
Hours: The park is open throughout the year.
Admission: $4.00 per car from Memorial Day through Labor Day; free otherwise. Camping is $11.00 per night.
Best time to visit: Summer is the most popular time and also the most crowded. Late spring or early fall is also a good time to enjoy warm weather and avoid crowds.
Activities: Fishing, boat ramp, camping, saltwater pool and bathhouse, winter cross-country skiing.
Concessions: Snack bar.
Pets: Not allowed.
For more information:
    Heckscher State Park, East Islip, NY 11730; 516-581-4433.
    Campsite reservations, 800-456-CAMP.

Catskills/
Hudson Valley

BEAR MOUNTAIN STATE PARK

A foot and light-hearted I take to the open road,
Healthy, free, the world before me,
The long brown path before me leading wherever I choose.

Henceforth I ask not good-fortune, I myself am good-fortune,
Henceforth I whimper no more, postpone no more, need nothing,
Done with indoor complaints, libraries, querulous criticisms,
Strong and content I travel the open road.

This opening from Walt Whitman's "Song of the Open Road" is carved on a huge boulder next to a larger-than-life statue of the famed American poet. The statue and boulder are on Bear Mountain State Park's Nature Trail.

The statue was erected in honor of Mrs. E. H. Harriman, who rescued Bear Mountain and the surrounding lands from one of the dumbest ideas ever – building a prison on top of Bear Mountain. Specifically, the New York State Prison Commission wanted to build Sing Sing Prison on this isolated parcel of land along the Hudson River. The fact that the prison would appropriate one of the best vistas in the scenic Hudson Valley seemed not to bother the commissioners.

The public, however, was outraged and protested loudly – inspired in part by the spirit of then President Theodore Roosevelt, a New Yorker and the most ardent conservationist who ever lived in the White House. Mrs. Harriman came to the rescue with the offer of 10,000 acres of land in Orange and Rockland Counties and $1,000,000 for the purchase of other nearby land. The offer was made on condition that the Bear Mountain site be scrapped and that the Palisades Interstate Park commissioners become the proposed new park's managers. The conditions were accepted. In 1910, Bear Mountain and adjoining Harriman State Park were created.

Palisades Interstate Park was established in 1900 to save the Palisades cliffs along the Hudson River from further exploitation. The area had been heavily quarried during the latter half of the nineteenth century. At the turn of the century the New York and New Jersey legislatures authorized the Palisades Park commission to acquire territory in order to preserve the picturesque cliffs that border the Hudson River in both states.

In 1609 Henry Hudson, an English navigator engaged by the Dutch East India Company to find a northwest passage to China, became the first European to sail up this river. Here in Bear Mountain Park, it's easy to see what invited the famed navigator's exploration. Even here, forty-four miles upstream from New York City, the river is still an arm of the sea. Its waters rise and fall with the ocean tides. The Mohican Indians called the river Muhheakunnuk, "great waters constantly in motion."

Bear Mountain State Park and adjacent Harriman State Park are two of the largest and oldest parks in the Palisades region. Standing atop Bear Mountain on a very clear day, you can see Manhattan's skyline forty-five miles to the south. Even if your view doesn't include Manhattan, it will include the Hudson River, Bear Mountain Bridge, and neighboring mountains and valleys. The top of Bear Mountain is 1,305 feet above sea level – certainly not up to the standards of the Rockies or even the Adirondacks to the north, but quite respectable by metropolitan New York standards.

Perkins Memorial Drive leads to the top of Bear Mountain, where Perkins Memorial Tower offers a higher elevation and even more spectacular views for those who wish to make the climb. Many hikers enjoy a jaunt up the mountain along the 3.3-mile Major Welch Trail, which is suitable for all levels of hikers. The entrance is behind the Bear Mountain Inn, and the climb parallels the western shore of Hessian Lake. The final 800 feet of the trail takes hikers up a steep slope to the top. There are splendid views throughout the walk – although the best is definitely at the top.

Bear Mountain and Harriman Parks have an extensive trail system. Pick up a trail map in the park office. There are trails to fit all levels of hikers, including the 4.3-mile Popolopen Gorge Trail, which follows a brook and a gorge by that name; the challenging 20.8-mile Ramapo-Dunderberg Trail; and the rugged 24.3-mile Suffern–Bear Mountain Trail. The Appalachian Trail also passes through the park.

Part of the Appalachian Trail passes through the Bear Mountain Nature Trail and Trailside Museum. The self-guided Bear Mountain Trail is the oldest continuously run trail in the country. We immediately felt the refreshing coolness of shade cast by the towering hardwoods. The zoo is filled with an unusual assortment of mostly rescued birds and mammals indigenous to the area.

We watched bears frolicking and had the opportunity to feel the jaw and examine the teeth of a bear who died at the zoo many years ago. The jaw was offered to us by a zoo volunteer who particularly enjoys engaging young visitors in discussions about bear teeth. The bear den has the distinction of being the lowest point on the Appalachian Trail: 115.4 feet above sea level.

Just beyond the bear's den, we looked into the forest about 100 feet from our path to see a large buck deer with a magnificent set of antlers still covered in velvet. He, like us, was just visiting, although the staff said they had seen him daily for the last week. Deer seem to be plentiful in the park—we had seen several young does and a fawn the day before.

We also saw Lefty, the one-winged peregrine falcon; Cody, an eastern coyote who, as a pup, followed a local German shepherd home; and Sam, a northern bald eagle. There's a beaver lodge that has been cut away for easy viewing; deer; a reptile house; and trees, shrubs, and plants with identification tags.

The trailside museum is composed of several buildings—compact and yet filled with an amazing array of exhibits and artifacts—all designed to tell the history, geology, and natural history of the area. There are rocks, pottery, arrowheads—even a mastodon that was found nearby. The historical museum is on the site of old Fort Clinton, which was stormed and captured by the British during the Revolution.

There are no motors on pristine Hessian Lake, but there are paddleboats and rowboats for rent and smallmouth bass for the lucky angler. For swimmers, there's a huge, 94- x 224-foot swimming pool set amidst gigantic boulders, so that it looks as if it had been carved out of the cliffs. The park also has picnic groves, a large playfield, basketball courts, and nature trails. During the winter there are ski jumps, sledding, ice skating, Christmas festivals, crafts shows, and winter carnivals.

The Bear Mountain Inn, a massive stone and wood structure dating from 1914, hosts meetings, banquets, conferences, and seminars as well as overnight guests. The stone fireplaces are gigantic—real walk-in fireplaces. There are guestrooms on the third floor as well as four stone lodges with six individual bedrooms each. The lodges are about one mile from the inn. The second Friday in December marks the beginning of the Bear Mountain Christmas Festival. Trees are decorated, Santa is in residence, and handmade crafts, gingerbread houses, and folk art fill the inn. The Overlook Lodge, on the opposite side of Hessian Lake, also offers rooms.

Where: Bear Mountain State Park is forty-five miles from New York City. Take US 9W or exit 14 off the Palisades Interstate Parkway.

Hours: The park is open year-round from 8:00 A.M. to dusk.

Admission: The park is free, although there are fees for various activities, including swimming. There is a $3.00 parking fee.

Best time to visit: Winter for skiing; spring for wildflowers; summer for swimming, boating, and cool mountain trails; early October for leaf color.

Activities: Fishing, swimming, hiking, skiing, skating, museum.

Pets: Dogs only, muzzled and on a leash. No pets in swimming area, buildings, or picnic areas.

For more information:

Bear Mountain State Park, Bear Mountain, NY 10911; 914-786-2701.

Bear Mountain Inn, 914-786-2731.

CATSKILLS FISHING

Fishing is regarded with near-religious fervor among many visitors and local residents in the Catskills. It has been said that God created the Catskills for the trout fisherman. Because of the high quality of the waters and the accessibility they offer to large populations, the Catskills became the region where dry fly fishing was introduced to America and where it flourishes today.

The geology of the Catskill Mountains creates ideal trout-stream conditions. Rounded slopes with deep-cut ravines, elevations favoring shady evergreens, and boulder-laden, smooth-gravel waterways create a combination of mountainous elements that promote environmental perfection. The Catskills were built layer upon layer from sedimentary deposits in a great inland sea that covered this area millions of years ago.

There are more than 500 miles of prime trout streams in the Catskills. When all tributaries are taken into account, the total is many, many times this mileage. Some of the streams are world-famous. Despite their closeness to New York City, they provide quiet, uncrowded trout fishing at its best. Of course, you can expect elbow-to-elbow fishing just about everywhere in the Catskills on April 1, the first day of trout season.

Most of the major trout streams are within Catskill Park. Watersheds inside its boundaries contribute to the flow of the Hudson, Delaware, and Mohawk river systems. Esopus Creek, with its excellent trout water, is a tributary of the Hudson. Schoharie Creek flows into the Mohawk. The Neversink, Beaver Kill, Willowemoc, East Branch, and West Branch belong to the Delaware River drainage system. These are the main trout streams of the Catskills. All of these waterways are included in New York State's "fishiest fifty" trout streams.

In addition to the wondrous trout streams, the Catskills boast another unique fishing resource – New York City's water reservoirs. Superior stream fishing is matched by a wealth of reservoir fishing in mountain settings that rival early settlement days. These unspoiled conditions are the result of a New York City policy of protecting its reservoirs with a sizable buffer zone of trees to the water's edge.

Six bodies of water make up this unusual reservoir system. They are the Ashokan, Cannonsville, Neversink, Pepacton, Rondout, and Schoharie reservoirs. These half-dozen reservoirs

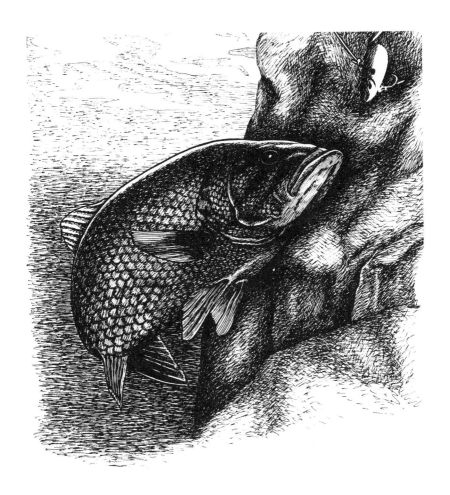

**Fish for bass in the morning or evening
when the weather is overcast and stable**

contain approximately forty square miles of high-quality fishing waters close to the nation's largest metropolitan area.

The reason for the pristine conditions and the unusually good fishing is that these waters are managed and protected as the purest, cleanest drinking supplies known to modern technology. Every year at the state fair in Syracuse, New York City rates among the top municipal water systems in taste tests. Two agencies control the policies that govern access and use of New York City reservoirs in the Catskills as a sport fishing resource. One is the Board of Water Supply. The other is the Department of Water Supply, Gas and Electricity. It is the department's duty "to preserve the purity of all water from which any part of the city's water supply is drawn, and to protect such supplies and the lands adjacent thereto from injury or nuisance." The agency's rules and regulations are designed to guide the fisherman's conduct and activities while he or she is a guest of New York City enjoying fishing in the reservoirs.

Bathing, swimming, and wading are prohibited in the reservoirs, as are all boats except rowboats with a special permit. Boats must be inspected and receive a permit before they can be launched. In addition to a New York State Fishing License, fishermen need a special reservoir permit, which is free. In addition, all reservoirs have certain restricted areas where all access is prohibited.

Within the reservoirs, trout and bass attract most fishing enthusiasts. But walleye, yellow perch, and bullhead are also sought after. Sunfish, rock bass, and other panfish are in great abundance.

The Ashokan Reservoir was the first of New York City's Catskill reservoirs. On September 9, 1913, the gates were shut to allow water to start filling the immense, twenty-mile-long reservoir, which displaced thousands of people and drowned seven hamlets. Local legend claims that on a still day you can look into the reservoir and see the streets of one unfortunate town. Ashokan is in northeastern Ulster County, about seven miles west of Kingston and about 100 miles from New York City. From Kingston take State 28 west to the reservoir.

The reservoir has proved to be a top fish producer. At one time it held the state's brown-trout record—a fish weighing 19

FISHING SCHOOL

If you are a novice or beginning fly-fisherman, lessons at a fly-fishing school can speed up learning and greatly add to your enjoyment. The Beaverkill Angler School of Fly-Fishing in Roscoe (also known as Trout Town USA) offers a variety of classes along the banks of the legendary Willowemoc and Beaverkill Rivers.

One of the most popular classes is the one-day class for two. The class covers equipment use and selection, proper casting techniques, tying the basic knots, reading the water, fly presentation, food trout feed on, and fishing Catskill waters. Orvis rods and reels are provided free while you attend the school. Classes are generally held May through October.

For more information: Beaverkill Angler, Stewart Ave., PO Box 198, Roscoe, NY 12776; 607-498-5194.

---

pounds, 14 ounces. The most common fish in Ashokan are rainbow trout, brown trout, smallmouth bass, walleye, yellow perch, pickerel, rock bass, and sunfish. Popular fishing spots are the Dividing Weir and the Chimney Hole. The smallmouth bass is the number-one game fish in the reservoir. Sunken quarries, rocky shoals, and gravelly coves provide ideal feeding and breeding grounds for this fighter. Coming from the pure, sweet waters of Ashokan, the fish makes especially good eating.

Given the image of fly-fishing in the Catskills, it is natural that there be a museum here dedicated to the subject. The Catskill Fly-Fishing Center and Museum is on Old Route 17 on the Willowemoc Creek between Roscoe and Livingston Manor. It is open year-round, although demonstrations take place only on weekends in the summer. Admission is free.

The center and museum command a beautiful spot on the world-famous Willowemoc Creek. As the birthplace of fly-fishing in the United States, the creek attracts sportspeople from all over the world. The center was founded in 1978 as an educational source and offers classes in fly tying and fly-fishing during July and August for children as young as eight. The museum contains continually changing exhibits on the history and lore of fly-fishing.

Short tours of the grounds are provided. The casting pond and aquarium are fun stops for fishing enthusiasts of all ages. Roscoe's Broad Street—the main street—is lined with tackle shops. All have friendly and helpful salespeople so that you can outfit yourself and your family for a day's fishing on Willo-wemoc Creek.

For more information:

Catskill Fly-Fishing Center, RD 1, Box 130C, Old Route 17, Livingston Manor, NY 12758; 914-439-4810.

ICE CAVES MOUNTAIN

If heights unnerve you as they do me, stay away from the edges at Sam's Point on Ice Caves Mountain in the Shawangunks. But take a good look at a view that is breathtaking, especially on a clear day, when you can see five states.

There are safety walks here, but you will definitely feel suspended over the valley below. From Sam's Point, you can weave your way through the Pine Tree Maze. Sam's Point supposedly got its name from a trapper who, fleeing a Native American war party, jumped over the edge and landed safely in some trees.

Sam's Point, a registered national landmark, is a little less than half a mile above sea level on Ice Caves Mountain, a privately operated park. You get there by taking a road to the top of the mountain, then hiking the well-marked half-mile trail down the Stairway of Stone, past the River of Mystery, and through crevices created by the glacial ice millions of years ago, ending at the Ice Cave. The walk will take you past chasms and tunnels, around incredible balanced rocks, and into lighted caves with remarkable mineral formations.

Tours are self-guided through the use of signs and brochures as well as a free tape player. Explore at your own pace, but be sure to wear hiking shoes or sneakers. Bring a jacket or sweater.

Where: State 52, Ellenville in the Shawangunks.

Hours: Open daily May to November, weather permitting. Hours vary depending on the season. Generally 9:00 A.M. to dusk.

Admission: $6.00 for adults, $4.00 for children 6–12, under 6 free.

Best time to visit: Fall for the most spectacular colors in the mountains.

Activities: Hiking, picnicking, cave exploration.

Concessions: Gift shop, picnic area, and an 18-hole miniature golf course.

Pets: Dogs must be on a leash.

For more information:

Ice Caves Mountain, Box 430, Walker Valley, NY 12588; 914-647-7989.

MINNEWASKA STATE PARK

The Shawangunk Mountains don't have the name recognition of the Catskills just to the north, but they do offer spectacular vistas, miles of hiking trails, glistening lakes, and a lovely park – Minnewaska State Park.

Geologically, the Shawangunks are about 100 million years older than the Catskills. The "Gunks," as many people call them, are made of a durable, gleaming-white conglomerate that gives the ridge its special beauty. It forms sharp pinnacles, sheer cliffs, fields of huge boulders, and windswept knobs where only a few hardy plants maintain a foothold.

The northern part of the Shawangunk Mountain ridge is roughly triangular in shape with its most northern point in Rosedale, where stone for the base of the Statue of Liberty was quarried. The sides of the triangle are formed by the Rondout Creek valley in the west, which roughly parallels US 209, and by the Wallkill River valley in the east.

Everywhere there are lookout points and views. "Some of those vistas will take your breath away," says Peter Gulliver, park manager at Minnewaska State Park, an 11,000-acre preserve in the heart of the Shawangunk Mountain ridge. "Hikes are extremely pleasant, and most are the kind of thing mom and dad can do with the children and not be exhausted afterward. It's a wilderness experience, but one you can get by walking a couple of miles and then hopping back in your car. That's a treat."

The best part of coming to the park is making use of the superb network of walking and hiking trails. Pick up a free trail map at the park's information booth. Just past the booth to your left is a carriageway. A few minutes' walk down this path brings you to Awosting Falls, where the foaming waters of the Peters Kill tumble over a sheer cliff into a deep pool.

If you have children or are just looking for a short hike, take the Beacon Hill Trail, a gently rolling carriageway on which you could push a baby stroller. About a two-mile round trip from the parking area at Lake Minnewaska, Beacon Hill has a magnificent view of the Wallkill Valley.

For something longer, make the five-mile round trip on the Millbrook Mountain Trail. For an all-day experience, take the Castle Point Trail, then visit Lake Awosting, the largest lake in the Shawangunks, returning by either the Upper or Lower Awosting Trail, depending on where your car is parked.

The weather can change quickly in the mountains, so be prepared and bring a warm jacket. Open fire of any sort is strictly forbidden in the Shawangunks because of the flammable pitch pine and laurel.

Lake Minnewaska itself is surrounded by a network of woodland trails and carriageways that are excellent for hiking, horseback riding, and cross-country skiing. The paved carriageways are great for biking. Swimming is permitted at the sandy beach area of the lake, where a lifeguard is on duty. Lake Awosting also offers swimming, but this lake is about a three-mile walk from the entrance.

Where: US 44, just west of the village of Minnewaska, about 12 miles from New Paltz.

Hours: 9 A.M. to dusk daily, year-round.

Admission: $4.00 per car from late June through Labor Day, $3.00 per car during the spring and fall. During the winter the charges are per person for skiers: $4.00 for adults, $3.00 for under 17, and $2.00 for seniors 62 and over. On weekends and holidays the charges are $5.00 for adults and seniors and $4.00 for under 17.

Best time to visit: Each season has something special to offer. Fall can be especially lovely at Minnewaska. During the winter the park trails are popular with cross-country ski enthusiasts.

Activities: Hiking, swimming, picnicking, cross-country skiing, horseback riding. No overnight camping.

Concessions: Snack bar, ski rental.

Pets: Dogs only, and they must be on a leash. No pets in swimming areas.

For more information:

Minnewaska State Park, PO Box 893, New Paltz, NY 12561; 914-255-0752.

CATSKILL PARK

Although the Catskills are nowhere near the highest of American mountains, they are the most visited, painted, and written about of all the country's mountain ranges. Much of their fame is due to their proximity to New York City and the millions of people who leave the city looking for a nearby respite and an escape to nature.

The Catskills have many faces: the borscht-belt Catskills, home to Grossinger's and other famous Jewish resorts; the fly-fishing Catskills, home to some of America's most renowned trout streams; the hiking Catskills; and the Catskills of old, filled with history and romance.

It was Washington Irving who brought the romance of the mountain region to the world, in his 1819 *Tale of Rip Van Winkle*. "These fairy mountains," as Irving called them, took on a new image through the story. Their old and worn appearance adds to their romantic aura.

The mountains did not result from violent crumplings of the earth's surface. They achieved their present form through eons of erosion. A succession of ice sheets covered the Catskills until some 15,000 years ago, leaving the region gouged and scraped, with sand and gravel heaped up and valleys turned into lakes.

All this activity produced Slide Mountain, at 4,204 feet the Catskills' highest summit. It also created a rocky wall 2,000 feet high facing miles of the Hudson River, with a tableland above and many mountains of 2,500 to 3,700 feet.

During the nineteenth century, the riches of the region were ruthlessly exploited. Forest fires frequently raged on mountainsides covered with debris from the hasty removal of the saleable parts of trees. Concerned citizens began to agitate for the creation of the Catskill Forest Preserve to hold and protect the water supply of area towns and cities and to restore the integrity of the fabled trout streams.

The Catskill (and the Adirondack) Forest Preserve was created on May 15, 1885, when Governor David B. Hill signed a law requiring that "all the lands now owned or which may hereafter be acquired by the State of New York . . . in three Catskill and eleven Adirondack counties . . . be forever kept as wild forest lands. They shall not be sold nor shall they be leased or taken by any person or corporation, public or private."

In 1888, Delaware County was added to the list of three counties in which the state lands constituted the Catskill Forest Preserve. The same four-county listing—Delaware, Greene, Sullivan, and Ulster—continues today. In 1892 the first allocation, in the sum of $250, was made to construct a "public path" in the Forest Preserve. It was for a trail to the summit of Slide Mountain, the highest mountain in the Catskills. From this small beginning has evolved a major recreational network consisting of trails for hiking, horseback riding, skiing, and snowmobiling.

In the 1916 and 1924 general elections, bond issues added nearly 121,000 acres to the Catskill Forest Preserve. More lands have been added over the years until, today, the Catskill Forest Preserve constitutes more than thirty-eight percent of the total area of Catskill Park. New York's forest preserve in the Catskills and Adirondacks presents an impressive example of forest preservation to the world. Encompassing the largest wilderness east of the Mississippi River, it has the distinction of being protected by a specific article in New York's constitution.

When Catskill Park was created in 1904, it included a total of 576,120 acres. The boundaries of the new park were shown on a map by a blue line, a delineation in keeping with a tradition begun with the establishment of Adirondack Park in 1892. Like Adirondack Park, Catskill Park includes towns and development within its boundaries. This mixture of private and public lands has produced an ongoing controversy over the forces of development. In 1957 Catskill Park was enlarged on the east to include Ashokan Reservoir and on the south

**Porcupines will eat just about anything that tastes salty—
even gloves and canoe paddles**

to include additional acres of Sullivan and Delaware Counties, for a total of 705,500 acres. In 1985, under a Catskill Park Master Plan, the park was divided into different classifications, including four wilderness areas totaling more than 92,000 acres.

The creation of the forest preserve helped the mountain

region maintain and restore the charm that Washington Irving first made known to the world. The Catskills are still the land of Rip Van Winkle, and they can still play tricks on one's sense of time and place.

One of the most spectacular and special views in all the Catskills is the site of the Catskill Mountain House, a hotel that is no more, in the northeastern corner of Catskill Park. Take State 32 to Palenville and then follow State 23A to Haines Falls. Take a right on State 18 at the sign for North Lake State Campsite. At North Lake you can get a map to the Mountain House Site.

Though the building is gone, the view remains, an enduring and enchanting vista. James Fenimore Cooper called it "the greatest wonder of all creation." Artist Thomas Cole, founder of the Hudson River School and a resident of nearby Catskill, felt that this "grand diorama" was far too sublime for him to paint. They were talking about the view from the then-world-famous Catskill Mountain House, certainly one of the most beloved hotels in nineteenth-century America.

The hotel started in 1823 when Erastus Beach, a stagecoach operator, built a small inn called Pine Orchard on the Wall of Manitou, a rock ledge 2,500 feet above the Hudson Valley. It was expanded over the years and in its final form was a magnificent Greek Revival structure with 300 rooms. Everyone who was anyone stayed here. The hotel lasted into the twentieth century, but then fell into a slow decline. The last guest left in 1942. On January 25, 1963, the state said the building was in a dangerous condition and burned it to the ground. Today all that is left is a commemorative marker on the site.

And there is the view. Ah, what a view — even for someone such as myself, with a fear of heights. There is a deep peace and quiet here. Many have invoked the Creator after experiencing this panorama. Take the time to walk along the escarpment to enjoy the differing vistas and to watch the changes in the light patterns.

Just a short distance away is Kaaterskill Falls, which Washington Irving called "wild, lovely and shagged." The falls are in North and South Lakes, a campground and recreational area operated by the New York State Department of Environmental Conservation. This campground offers some spectacular scenery and a multitude of activities. If you hike around the lakes, keep your eyes open for the "lost treasure of Rip Van Winkle." This is a gem-encrusted ebony ninepin that will go to the finder of a stone inscribed with Van Winkle's initials. Whoever finds the treasure stone, which is located on public land somewhere in Green County, can claim the treasure.

A short hike through the woods will bring you to Kaaterskill Falls, one of the highest falls on the East Coast. During the late eighteenth and early nineteenth centuries, this out-of-the-way area occupied a central place in the American mind because it represented pure, savage, beautiful wilderness, which Americans had in abundance and Europe did not. At the time, other spectacular sights were either too remote or still undiscovered. But the Catskills were and are both accessible and remote, especially here in Kaaterskill Falls.

Natty Bumppo in James Fenimore Cooper's *The Pioneers* describes the high, narrow falls:

"There the water comes crooking and winding among the rocks; first so slow that a trout could swim in it, and then starting and running like a creature that wanted to make a far spring, till it gets to where the mountain divides, like the cleft hoof of a deer, leaving a deep hollow for the brook to tumble into . . . . To my judgment, lad, it's the best piece of work that I've met with in the woods; and none know how often the hand of God is seen in the wilderness, but them that rove it for a man's life."

Miraculously, the falls and the surrounding area have changed little since Cooper's day. There's a clean, sandy beach with lifeguards, boat rental (no motors allowed), a snack bar, changing rooms, and 219 campsites. Some of the campsites are handicapped accessible.

Where: From New York City, 87N to Exit 20 to 32N to State 23A to County 18 (O'Hara Road) in Haines Falls.
Hours: Daily 9:00 A.M. to dusk, May to the beginning of December.
Admission: $4.00 per car for day use during the summer; camping $10.00 per night.
Best time to visit: The rate of water flow at the falls is the highest in the spring after the rains and snow melt. Weekends can be crowded during the summer.
Activities: Camping, hiking, swimming, boating.
Pets: Allowed on a leash with proof of rabies vaccination.
For more information:
    North and South Lakes, Haines Falls, NY 12436; 518-589-5058.
    For a campsite reservation, 800-456-CAMP.

HUNTER MOUNTAIN

Just a few miles to the west is Hunter Mountain, the "snow-making capital of the world." The ski resort was born January 9, 1960, defying expert advice that the mountain would never become a major ski center. Since that day, millions of skiers have skied Hunter Mountain. The average ski season is 162 days. Most of the construction work was done by Israel and Orville Slutzky, who have been the operators and geniuses behind the success of Hunter almost from the beginning. The brothers are the "Mister Inside and Mister Outside" of the ski business. Issy is outside skiing every day of the season and keeping an eagle eye on trail conditions and the weather. Orville is inside with a bank of forty television screens that show him almost the entire mountain.

Hunter Mountain was the first ski area in the country to offer 100-percent snowmaking, the first to offer top-to-bottom snowmaking, and the first in the United States to install an automated snowmaking system. Hunter's snowmaking expertise and equipment have been loaned to others, including the 1980 Lake Placid Winter Olympics.

Not content with their long ski season, the brothers have turned the resort into a multiple-season center of activity. There's the Patriot Festival, the German Alps Festival, the Hunter Country Music Festival, Rockstalgia, the International Celtic Festival with a spectacular march by 700 bagpipers and drummers, the National Polka Festival, the Mountain Eagle Indian Festival, and Oktoberfest. The chairlifts, the highest in the Catskills, operate during the fall foliage season to offer splendid views during late September and October.

Where: State 23A, Hunter.
Hours: Ski season, generally November through April, with daily skiing, including nights.
Best time to visit: Weekends naturally are the most crowded. Come in the fall for leaf peeping and in the summer for ethnic festivals.
Activities: Skiing on forty-seven slopes and trails, with fifteen lifts and tows; specialty races and promotions, including races for firefighters, police, nurses, chefs, doctors, ad people, and many more (it was here that the 70-plus Skiers Club was founded and still meets annually for a day on the slopes); cross-country skiing.
Concessions: a restaurant, ski museum, and liftside condos; a ski shop and ski school; child care and special lessons for young children.
Pets: Not allowed.

For more information:
   Hunter Mountain, Hunter, NY 12442; 518-263-4223.
   Snow information, 800-FOR-SNOW.
   Summer festival information, 800-367-7669.
   Hunter Mountain Ski Bowl Reservations, 800-775-4641.
   Catskill Park information, 800-642-4443 for Delaware County, 800-542-2414 for Green County, 800-882-CATs for Sullivan County, and 800-DIAL UCO for Ulster County.

3

Finger Lakes and Central New York

WATKINS GLEN

"We are about to leave human time altogether and go far, far back into the geologic past—almost a million times 5,000 years. We are going back to a time when the earth was young—over four and one half billion years ago. . . ."

The haunting voice of the narrator begins the story of the creation of Watkins Glen as vivid laser lights dance off waterfalls and cliffs and sounds imitate erupting volcanoes, crackling ice, and the rhythmic beating of the Senecas' drums. We are witnessing Timespell, a sound and light show. It is a stirring performance set against a spectacular stage—the gorge of Watkins Glen State Park.

Watkins Glen is the most famous of the parks of the Finger Lakes region, in western New York, an area known for its gorges and waterfalls. Every evening from mid-May through mid-

October Timespell takes over the glen at dusk and takes the audience back eons to the very beginning of the gorge.

The narrator's voice bridges the time from the dawn of the gorge's formation to the Ice Age, the thriving Seneca Indian communities here a few hundred years ago, and the first tourists in the mid-nineteenth century. The railroad that brought them here threatened to charge extra for women wearing more than twenty petticoats, we are told.

We learn of a time when this part of our country was made up of mountains as high as the Himalayas—all of them under the sea.

The public has been marveling at the glen's sculptured chasm and nineteen glistening waterfalls for more than a century. Opened to the public in 1863 by Morvalden Ells, a journalist from Elmira, the gorge was privately owned and operated as a tourist resort until it was purchased by the state of New York in 1906. It's at the tip of thirty-five-mile-long Seneca Lake, the deepest of the Finger Lakes and one of the deepest bodies of water in the United States.

Glen Creek has poured down the glacially steepened valleyside ever since, slowly eroding this gorge, a process that continues to this very moment.

The best way to experience the beauty of the glen is to hike the gorge trail. This trail and others are accessible from the main, south, and upper entrances. Most visitors walk uphill from the main entrance and return. Others take a shuttlebus to the upper entrance and walk the one and a half miles back down to the main entrance. Many prefer the shortened trip from the south entrance to the main or vice versa.

The trail has more than 800 stone steps. It is not a difficult walk, but the footing can get slippery, so be sure to wear suitable footwear.

Numbered markers along the trail refer to entries in the trail leaflet. There are nineteen waterfalls, bearing, names such as Rainbow, Diamond, and Pluto, and a series of grottos, caves, and cataracts. You'll pass through handcut tunnels, the "narrows" with its microclimate almost like that of a rainforest, and under and over bridges.

In the broad Cathedral area are two trails — Lovers' Lane and Indian Trail. Just where Lovers' Lane joins the Gorge Trail, there's a slab of stone with a ripple surface. Stand on it. You are standing on an ancient sea bottom. The ripples were formed in sand and silt on the floor of the sea that once covered much of New York State.

Central Cascade, which plunges more than sixty feet, is the highest waterfall in the gorge. The deep pools below these falls and elsewhere in the gorge were formed by the swirling of sand and stones wearing away at the tough siltstone in the stream bed.

At Rainbow Falls, rainbows can often be seen. Beyond the falls is Spiral Gorge, with pools and narrow Pluto Falls, named for the darkness of this portion of the Glen. Pluto was the Greek god of the underworld.

After you have walked the gorge you can hike one of several other marked trails or relax by the side of the fifty-meter pool. There are 302 campsites divided into villages named in honor of the Native Americans who lived in the area — Seneca Village, Onondaga Village, Oneida Village, Mohawk Village, Cayuga Village, and Tuscarora Village. Besides the main pool there is a children's pool, a recreation building, picnic areas, a snack bar, a gift shop, a playground, and playing fields.

Where: The main entrance is located on State 14 (Franklin Street) in the town of Watkins Glen at the tip of Seneca Lake.
Hours: It is open year-round, but the camping area and Gorge Trail are open from mid-May to Columbus Day.
Admission: $4.00 per car during the summer season. The camping rate is $10.00 per night. The cost of Timespell is $5.25 for

adults and $4.75 for children 6–11 and seniors 62 and over; children under six are free.

Best time to visit: May through the October season when the Gorge Trail and Timespell are open. The park is open for hiking, cross-country skiing, and snowmobiling during the winter.

Activities: Hiking, sound and light show, camping, swimming, picnicking, playground, playing fields.

Pets: Allowed on a leash with proof of rabies vaccination.

For more information:

Watkins Glen State Park, PO Box 304, Watkins Glen, NY 14891; 607-535-4511, or 607-535-4960 for Timespell.

BUTTERMILK FALLS STATE PARK

If you've ever dreamed of jumping into an old-time swimming hole, Buttermilk Falls State Park is the place for you. These are falls that refresh rather overwhelm. A natural spring-fed pool at the base of the falls is cool and relaxing on a hot summer day.

Buttermilk Creek has poured down the steep side of the valley since the Ice Age, forming the long cascade from which the park takes its name. Thousands of years of erosion in the native shale and sandstone have left waterfalls, high cliffs, sculptured pools, and Pinnacle Rock.

During the 1700s, Sapony Indians lived in the village of Coreorgonel near Buttermilk Falls. There were twenty-five log cabins surrounded by cultivated fields and plum and apple orchards. The inhabitants of Coreorgonel fled before the arrival of Colonel Dearborn and 200 men of Gen. John Sullivan's Continental Army during the Revolutionary War. The army burned Coreorgonel on September 4, 1779.

Early European settlers constructed dams and mills along Buttermilk Creek. There was once an old mill at the base of the gorge. Van Orman's Dam was built in the gorge in 1872 and

**A young raccoon peeks from the safety of its nest
in a hollow tree**

supplied water to Ithaca until 1903. The dam no longer exists.

Between 1912 and 1920 the movie industry flourished in Ithaca, as the gorges were backdrops for many films. Some segments of *The Perils of Pauline* were filmed in Buttermilk Glen.

In 1924, Robert and Laura Treman donated 154 acres in Buttermilk Glen to New York for a state park. The park has since been enlarged to 751 acres.

Cool trails take hikers uphill and alongside Buttermilk Creek, which drops more than 500 feet in a series of cascades and rapids. In all there are ten waterfalls and two glens.

The park has sixty campsites—no utilities; RVs are allowed. There are seven cabins, a bathhouse by the pool, hiking trails, a playground and playing fields, picnic areas, nature trails, a concession stand, and a camper recreation program.

Where: The main entrance is on State 13, two miles south of Ithaca.

Hours: Open daily.

Admission: $4.00 per car during the summer season.

Best time to visit: On a hot summer day, when a plunge in the natural pool at the base of the falls is utterly refreshing.

Activities: Camping, swimming, hiking, picnicking, playgrounds, playing fields, nature walks.

Pets: Allowed on a leash with proof of rabies vaccination.

For more information:

Buttermilk Falls State Park, RD 10, Ithaca, NY 14850; 607-273-5761.

Campsite reservations, 800-456-CAMP.

HIGHLAND PARK

Is there any more heavenly aroma on earth than the delicate fragrance of the lilac? Rochester's Highland Park is world famous for its Lilac Festival, a ten-day celebration held every year in mid-May.

Lilacs grow abundantly throughout New York State, but nowhere are there more varieties than in Rochester's premier park. Traced to a province of China between Tibet and Mongolia, lilacs came to America with the early settlers. The flowering shrubs adapted well to life in the United States. They are hardy, need little care, and were a source of great pleasure in Colonial gardens. Both Thomas Jefferson and George Washington wrote of the lilacs in their gardens.

Highland Park was established in 1888. Four years later the park's first lilacs were planted by John Dunbar, a trained horticulturist from Long Island who had been brought to Rochester to oversee Highland Park. His first plantings consisted of twenty varieties; today more than 500 varieties cover twenty-two of the park's 155 acres.

New varieties have extended blooming times so that some of the lilacs flower well into June. The color range has broadened from pure white through delicate lavender to deepest purple.

Although the lilacs are the centerpiece of the park and the festival, they are set off by other May-blooming flowers, including azaleas, rhododendrons, magnolias, tulips, and a bed of 10,000 pansies. A quiet section of the park with a wrought-iron gateway leads to Poets' Walk—a shaded pathway through the woods.

Lamberton Conservatory on the park grounds was designed in 1911 along the lines of a Victorian greenhouse. It presents five major displays throughout the year. During the Lilac Festival, an information booth located nearby provides a daily schedule of events, including concerts and parades, and tours of the park, the lilac collection, and the Garden Center. Highland Park Bowl in the park is an outdoor amphitheater where concerts and plays are presented.

Although Rochester is probably best known as the home of Eastman Kodak, it is also known as "Flower City" and was internationally known for its nurseries. Highland Park got its start with twenty-two acres presented to the city by George Ellwanger and Patrick Barry, owners of the world-famous Ellwanger and Barry Nursery Company. The gift included a specimen of each kind of plant material from their nursery. In addition, plants from many American and European nurseries have made the park one of the horticultural centers of the world.

Where: Entrances at South Goodman Street, Highland Avenue, and Mount Hope Avenue in Rochester.
Hours: Highland Park is open daily. Lamberton Conservatory is open daily 9:00 A.M. to 5:00 P.M. except Mondays.
Admission: Free.
Best time to visit: Although flowers bloom throughout the growing season, mid-May to early June should reward the visitor with the beauty and aroma of the lilac.
Activities: Nature walk, greenhouse displays, Lilac Festival.
Pets: Allowed on a leash.
For more information:
The Greater Rochester Visitors Association, 126 Andrews Street, Rochester, NY 14604-1102; 716-546-3070.

TAUGHANNOCK FALLS

It is said that *Taughannock* means "great fall in the woods." Others believe the falls were named after a Delaware chief, Taughannock, whose body was thrown over the falls after a battle with the Iroquois.

Taughannock Falls, 215 feet high, is the highest vertical waterfall in the eastern United States — higher even than Niagara

Falls. The falls are part of a state park with the same name that includes more than a mile of Cayuga Lake shore, near Ithaca in western New York.

Archaeologists have discovered evidence of Native American villages on Taughannock Point. In 1677, an Englishman named Wentworth Greenhalgh wrote of a flourishing town on the point where Cayuga and Seneca Indians grew corn, beans, and Indian potatoes and tended an old apple orchard.

The Cayugas and Senecas, allies of the British, left the area following the Revolutionary War. The first white settler came to the area in 1790. Later, in the nineteenth century, a railroad station was constructed near the upper gorge, upstream from the falls. Sandstone was quarried upstream, shaped in a mill near the tracks, and shipped to New York City to make sidewalks.

Luxury hotels were built on either side of the gorge near the falls. Spacious Taughannock House was located where the parking lot for the falls overlook is today. Cataract House lay on the rim of the opposite cliff. Vacationers traveled to the hotels by steamboat and later by railroad from the 1860s to the early part of this century, when the golden age of luxury resorts in upstate New York came to an end. The hotels are long gone.

There are two falls lookout points: one from below at the end of the Gorge Trail, the other from above at the Falls Overlook on Taughannock Park Road. You can reach the base by walking along a gentle three-quarter-mile trail. Pick up a Gorge Trail brochure in the park office and follow the numbered markers, which correspond to those described in the brochure.

Stand at the beginning of the trail. Had you been at this spot two million years ago, you'd have been under hundreds of feet of stone; 20,000 years ago you'd have been under half a mile of ice; and 10,000 years ago you'd have been standing on the shore of Cayuga Lake right next to the falls. Now the falls are almost a mile away. Stop at marker No. 2 to see evidence of the waterfall's power. The constant pouring of water has gradually eaten away the rock supporting it. The same principle applies to super-sized Taughannock Falls, which has sculpted the gorge.

Marker No. 7 could be called "a little piece of Canada." The boulder was brought here by the most recent glacier, probably from Canada, during the Ice Age. Boulders of this type are known as "glacial erratics" and are quite common. Their presence at sites far from their origins is one of the clues that led to the theory of the Ice Age.

Taughannock Falls is at marker No. 8. It was spring during our latest visit, and the falls were roaring with the runoff from heavy winter snows and spring rains. During the summer the falls are quieter and the flow greatly reduced. The flat, easy walk goes through a rugged canyon and quiet woods, along a peaceful stream to the falls.

The park is 783 acres with seventy-six campsites (sixteen electric, sixty with no utilities). There are also sixteen cabins, a boat launch, docks, a swimming beach on the lake, a bathhouse, playgrounds and playing fields, a concession stand, camper recreation programs, and a summer music festival. Boat rentals are available.

Remember that the process of gorge formation continues today as rocks constantly erode and fall from the face of the falls and the gorge walls. Visitors are reminded to stay on the marked trails.

Where: The entrance is on State 89, eight miles north of Ithaca, near Trumansburg.

Hours: The park is open all year. Camping is available from the last weekend in March to mid-October.

Admission: $4.00 per car during the summer season; otherwise free.

Best time to visit: Spring if you wish to see the falls at their most impressive. The gorge and trails are especially lovely in the fall when the leaves turn.

Activities: Camping, boating, swimming, hiking, sledding, skating, playgrounds, playing fields.

Pets: Must be on a leash. Proof of rabies vaccination is required for all state parks.

For more information:

Taughannock Falls State Park, 2221 Taughannock Park Road, Trumansburg, NY 14886; 607-387-6739.

Campsite reservations, 800-456-CAMP.

CORNELL PLANTATIONS

From early spring until late fall blooms can always be found at the 1,500-acre Cornell Plantations, a unit of Cornell University that includes the Arboretum, Botanical Garden, and Natural Areas.

The primary purpose of the unit is to preserve Cornell's great natural heritage as a living resource and to enhance its value as an outdoor laboratory for the natural sciences. There are miles of trails.

The Plantations were the dream of Liberty Hyde Bailey, often called "the dean of American plant scientists." He described the Plantations as "a project which unites the study of wild, of economic, and of ornamental plants, of trees, of farm crops and animals, and of wildlife—things that grow—with research in the development of better forms of plants and animals—all for the wider service of man."

The blooms begin in late April in the Wildflower Garden—part of the Rockwell Field Laboratory, a sixteen-acre area that was transformed in 1952 from a dumping ground into a peaceful wooded spot with a rippling stream. There are wildflower favorites here — trillium, hepatica, adder's tongue — as well as rare flowers such as bishop's cap and doll's eyes. Most of the trees and plants are labeled so that visitors may identify them easily.

One of the unique specialty gardens is the Walter C. Muenscher Poisonous Plants Garden, dedicated to the late Professor Muenscher, eminent Cornell botanist and author of a classic text on poisonous plants. The garden contains specimens that he gathered from the wild as well as many added later.

The Robinson York State Herb Garden has been designed to serve as a living reference library for herb study and research. Herb gardening and herb usage are increasing in popularity, and this garden has more than 800 herbs to be seen, studied, and enjoyed for their color, texture, and fragrance.

In the International Crop Garden you can study the nine major crops that feed the world. The Heritage Crop Garden showcases old-time crops. The Rhododendron and Peony Gardens are spectacular in late May and early June. A gift shop specializes in books on plants and horticulture.

Where: The Cornell Plantations are off Plantations Road, adjacent to Cornell University in Ithaca at the southern tip of Cayuga Lake.

Hours: Sunrise to sunset daily. Some trails and roads are closed in winter.

Admission: Free.

Best time to visit: Depends on your taste in flowers. The peony and rhododendron blossoms are so colorful and extravagant in late May and early June that a visit timed for their flowering would be a good choice.

Pets: Dogs are allowed on a short leash. Be prepared to clean up after your dog.

For more information:
Cornell Plantations, One Plantation Road, Ithaca, NY

14850, or call the gift shop at 607-255-3020 (8:00 A.M. to 4:00 P.M. weekdays year-round, 11:00 A.M. to 5:00 P.M. weekends April through December. Closed Sundays in November and December).

HOWE CAVERNS

Farmer Lester Howe wondered why his cows stood out in the hot sun near some bushes instead of under the shade trees as his neighbors' cows did. Upon investigation, he discovered cool air blowing up out of a cave entrance behind the bushes.

After thorough exploration, Howe named the cavern after himself and opened it to the public. The year was 1842. Soon heralded as a tourist attraction second only to Niagara Falls, the cave required a descent of eight to ten hours of climbing and wading for the intrepid tourists, who were provided oilskin coats and hats, rubber boots, lanterns, and a box lunch—all for fifty cents.

Today, an elevator takes visitors 156 feet to the subterranean walkway. From there your guide will lead the way through caverns with stalactites and stalagmites—well lit by spotlights.

You'll also receive a geology lesson. The stalactites and stalagmites are formed by dripping water that picks up small amounts of limestone and leaves it behind after the water evaporates.

Stalactites, which grow from the ceiling downward (the word is spelled with a "c," as in *ceiling*), form as dripping water deposits limestone particles. The process occurs over millions of years. Stalagmites, which grow from the ground upward (spelled with a "g," as in *ground*), are formed in a similar manner. Flowstone, a first cousin of stalactites and stalagmites, is a limestone deposit growing on cavern walls. It looks like sheets of rippling ice.

Only about one cubic inch of a limestone formation will develop in a hundred years. Our guide tells us that the caverns had their start about 6,000,000 years ago. At that time, this part of New York was covered by seawater.

Although several rocks look as though they are balanced precariously, they actually have been in place for millions of years. Mike, our guide, says it is estimated that the last rock fell in the caverns 10,000 years ago. Another isn't expected to fall for another 30,000 years.

It's always fifty-two degrees down below. It may not seem to be the perfect setting for a wedding, but more than 200 couples have tied the knot here, beginning with Lester Howe's daughter Elgiva, who did it as an early marketing stunt. There's even a heart-shaped calcite stone set in the Bridal Altar. Legend has it that if you are single and looking, you will be married within the year if you step on the heart-shaped stone.

At one point your guide will hum into a rock, producing sound that seems to come from stalactites and stalagmites that have grown together to form what is called the pipe organ. Then he will turn off all lights and you will be plunged into total, absolute darkness—a strange feeling, especially for those who have never experienced it before.

Next you will be invited to toss a coin into the subterranean wishing well. The money is collected regularly and given to charity.

"Hop into one of our luxury liners," our guide tells us. Howe Caverns has two twenty-two-passenger boats to carry visitors across the Lake of Venus, fed by the rushing water of the underground River Styx. Just before you reach the six-and-a-half-foot waterfall, the boats turn around and retrace their paths.

There's a snack bar and gift shop, an outside picnic area, and a twenty-four-room motel with a restaurant and a swimming pool. The motel is open from late April to mid-October. The motel is especially convenient if you are planning an underground wedding.

Where: Take the New York Thruway to exit 25A, then I-88 to exit 22. Take State 7 and follow the yellow signs. The travel time from exit 25A is approximately twenty-five minutes. The cave is thirty-seven miles from Albany and 160 miles from New York.

Hours: 9:00 A.M. to 6:00 P.M. daily except Thanksgiving, Christmas, and New Year's Day.

Admission: $10.50 for adults; $6.00 for children 7–12. Children six and under are free.

Best time to visit: Anytime. On hot summer days it is especially cool and refreshing inside the cave.

Activities: Cave exploration, picnicking, swimming.

Pets: Not allowed.

For more information:

Howe Caverns, Howes Cave, NY 12092; 518-296-8990.

FINGER LAKES NATIONAL FOREST

Purdy Corner, Breakneck Creek, Bumpus Corners, Cronk Cemetery, Cat Elbow Corner, Chickencoop Road—the names sound like places in an old Western movie. But they're not; they are a few of the surviving names in the post-Revolutionary War farmland that is now New York's only national forest.

The 13,232-acre Hector Ranger District, Finger Lakes National Forest, lies on a ridge between Seneca and Cayuga Lakes. The Iroquois were probably the first to inhabit the area. White settlers moved in to farm the land after the Revolutionary War. By 1900, soil depletion and increasing competition from the Midwest made farming in the area marginal.

During the Great Depression, the federal government stepped in to buy many farms and help relocate their residents. The farmland was put under Soil Conservation Service administration, and early management emphasized soil stabilization and conversion of cropland to pastures for domestic livestock grazing.

Finger Lakes National Forest is unique among public lands in the state for its long practice of multiple-use management. Some areas have been reforested, grazing areas have been established, and twenty-five ponds have been created to encourage waterfowl and to provide limited public fishing.

The 5,000-acre grazing program is unique in the East. Members of the Hector Cooperative Grazing Association bring their beef and dairy cattle to the pastures from May 15 to October 15.

The forest lands are open for hunting and fishing, with state licenses, as well as for hiking, cross-country skiing, horseback riding, and snowmobiling. The forest has more than twenty-five miles of connecting trails, including the twelve-mile Interlaken National Recreation Trail and two miles of the Finger Lakes Trail.

The trails are closed to motorized vehicles such as motorcycles and motorbikes. From small parking areas along the main trail, hikers may take loop trails that provide relaxing walks of half an hour up to four or five hours.

The forest has several special attractions. Backbone Trailhead is designed for picnicking or overnight camping by horseback riders. There are five acres of blueberries next to the Blueberry Patch Campground. The blueberries are native to the area, where they have been growing for centuries. The Cayuga and Seneca tribes used the berries fresh and also dried them for winter use.

For a small fee, the public may cut firewood for personal use in selected locations. Firewood permits may be obtained at the Forest Service office. The Potomac Group Campground is intended for the use of groups of ten to forty people. A fee is charged for reserved use of the site. Visitors may use the campground on a first-come, first-served basis if it is not reserved.

**Blueberries grow wild where the soil is acid and provide food
for bears, foxes, raccoons, and birds as well as people**

Two other small camping sites are available on a first-come,
first-served basis. Free camping is also allowed throughout the
forest.

Where: Finger Lakes National Forest is between Seneca and
Cayuga Lakes – four miles from Watkins Glen and seven miles
from Montour Falls.
Hours: Daily, year-round.
Admission: Free; fee for reserved camping.
Best time to visit: An especially beautiful time to visit is in late
May or early June when the wild pinxter and native azalea are in

riotous bloom; summer and fall are the most popular times to visit; cross-country skiers and snowmobilers enjoy the forest lands during the snow season.

Activities: Hiking, camping, fishing, hunting, cross-country skiing, horseback riding, snowmobiling.

Pets: Dogs must be on a leash.

For more information:

District Ranger, Hector Ranger District, Finger Lakes National Forest, 4588 State Route 224, Montour Falls, NY 14865; 607-594-2750.

MONTEZUMA NATIONAL WILDLIFE REFUGE

The Montezuma National Wildlife Refuge lies at the north end of Cayuga Lake in the heart of the Finger Lakes region. It was established in 1938 as a refuge and breeding ground for migratory birds and other wildlife as a unit of the Atlantic Flyway.

The region was shaped during the last glacial period, some 10,000 years ago, when the retreating glacier created a vast system of lakes. In time, the shallower northern and southern ends of the lakes developed into extensive marshes.

The earliest known inhabitants of the region were Algonquin Indians. They were succeeded by the Cayugas of the Iroquois Nation. These early Americans derived part of their livelihood from the wildlife and plants of the area's bountiful marshes.

Prior to the turn of the century, the Montezuma Marsh extended north from Cayuga Lake for twelve miles and was up to eight miles wide. The marsh was one of the most productive in North America. Unfortunately, as with most wetlands during that era, the importance of the marsh was unrecognized. Construction of a nearby dam and changes to rivers during the building of the New York State Barge Canal contributed to the loss of the marsh. By the early 1900s all but a few hundred acres had been drained.

In 1937 the Bureau of Biological Survey, which later became the U.S. Fish and Wildlife Service, purchased 6,432 acres of the former marsh. The Civilian Conservation Corps began work on a series of low dikes that would hold water and restore part of the marsh. Efforts to restore and preserve the marsh continue today.

Motorists crossing the state via the New York Thruway pass through the Montezuma Refuge. But it's hard to see much while driving along at highway speed. The refuge is worth a stop, especially for bird lovers. A total of 315 species of birds have been identified at the refuge since its establishment. While birds are in abundance year-round, it's best to time your visit for the fall or spring migration seasons to see hundreds of Canada geese, ducks, and snow geese.

On a first visit to a marsh, it takes some time to appreciate the landscape's unique characteristics. Areas appear almost lifeless, with acres of dead trees rising up like gaunt ghosts out of the murky waters. The trees died after the area was flooded to develop the marsh; the result is an excellent waterfowl habitat.

Stop first at the visitors center, where rangers are on duty to answer questions and provide up-to-date information on the latest sightings. There are birds on display here, as well as nests and eggs of the major birds found in the refuge. The observation deck and tower provide excellent opportunities to see wildlife.

During our last visit the highlight was the sight (through a telescope) of a bald eagle sitting on her nest. Bald eagles are on the endangered-species list. Prior to the 1950s, New York had about seventy nesting pairs of bald eagles. By 1960 there was only one known active bald-eagle nest.

Pesticides, primarily the now-banned DDT, are considered responsible for most of the eagles' decline. By the mid-1970s

**By the time they are three weeks old, most bald eaglets
have grown a thick, fuzzy coat of feathers**

New York had launched the most comprehensive bald-eagle restoration program in the nation, an effort designed to return breeding bald eagles to all portions of the state still suitable for their existence.

Since 1976, a total of twenty-three bald eagles have been released at the refuge. The project demonstrated that young bald

THE BALD EAGLE

The bald eagle is our nation's symbol and the only species of eagle unique to the North American continent. It is one of the largest birds of prey in North America. The males are three feet from head to tail, weigh eight to ten pounds, and have a wingspan of six and a half feet. The females are slightly larger, with a wingspan of up to eight feet. Immature eagles lack the white head and tail that characterize adult bald eagles.

Bald eagles live for twenty-five to thirty-five years in the wild. They usually mate for life; if one dies the other will seek a new mate. The birds reach reproductive maturity at four to five years of age.

The nests of bald eagles are large stick structures, usually high in large trees near water. Nests are reused and added to each year. After the first eaglets left the Montezuma nest in 1987, their nest was examined. The dead elm tree supporting the nest was found to be in very poor condition. Park personnel were concerned that the nest, precariously perched fifty feet up on an overhanging branch, would fall during winter storms or, even worse, during the spring when eggs or young were in the nest.

The refuge staff joined forces with the New York State Electric and Gas Corporation and the New York State Department of Environmental Conservation to stabilize the nest by installing a seventy-five-foot utility pole next to the nest tree. A cradle was positioned and bolted into place just under the nest. The utility company's linemen secured the nest to the platform. The trio of eagles produced one eaglet from the pole nest before building a new nest nearby in 1990. The trio of eagles has produced an average of two young per year since 1987.

Biologists believe that the future for the bald eagle in New York and at Montezuma looks very bright.

---

eagles can be reared in man-made situations and still learn to hunt, feed, and survive on their own. In July 1987 a local farmer reported seeing a large nest in an isolated location at the refuge. There were two young eaglets in the nest – the first to be produced at Montezuma in more than thirty years. An additional surprise came when a trio, rather than a pair, of eagles was observed tending to the young.

There are two observation towers in the refuge. One is just a short walk from the information center. A picnic area in a grove near the tower allows you to eat while watching birds and the vast expanse of marsh.

A drive along three-and-a-half mile Wildlife Drive is a good introduction to the world of the marsh. Pick up a brochure in the visitors center and follow the markers. Binoculars are useful.

Large numbers of Canada geese, snow geese, and ducks visit Montezuma during spring and fall, along with tundra swans. Ducks frequently seen are mallards, American black ducks, blue-winged and green-winged teal, American widgeon, northern shovelers, and wood ducks. Common diving ducks are canvasbacks, scaup, redheads, and common and hooded mergansers. Great blue herons, green-backed herons, American coots, common moorhens, bitterns, and other birds may often be seen along the drive.

Tschache Pool, 1,300 acres in size, is home to the bald eagles. Twenty-three eaglets have taken their first flights from the forty-foot platform overlooking the pool. There's an observation tower here.

Nearby is the Esker Brook Trail, a two-mile walking trail that is open year-round. The trail and the auto-tour route are open for cross-country skiing and snowshoeing during the winter.

Where: Five miles east of Seneca Falls. There is easy access from exits 40 or 41 of the New York Thruway, which crosses the refuge. For boaters, the Barge Canal system offers a convenient way of travel; May's Point Lock is within the refuge. Although fishing and boating are prohibited in refuge waters, the refuge maintains a boat launch providing access to the canal.

Three public fishing sites provide bank-fishing access to the canal.

Hours: Daily during daylight hours. The visitors center is staffed on weekends, most Tuesdays, and holidays.

Admission: Free.

Best time to visit: If you want to see great numbers of birds, visit during the peak time for migrations of Canada geese, which is mid-November. About 50,000 of the birds pass through the refuge in November. The peak time for ducks, which number up to 150,000, is late November. Best viewing times are early morning and late afternoon. The peak for shore birds is mid-September. During the winter, the auto route is generally closed to autos but open for cross-country skiing and snowshoeing. This is a good time to see white-tailed deer and resident birds. The spring migration is late February through April. About 85,000 Canada geese and 12,000 snow geese are in the refuge. Many ducks are present, although they are not as numerous as in the fall. The peak for wildflowers is May.

Activities: Bird and wildlife observation, visitors center, picnicking, scenic drives, cross-country skiing, snowshoeing. With advance notice, educational programs are available to organized groups throughout the year.

Pets: Must remain in car.

Other: The refuge provides an extensive assortment of films and videos to area educators. Films are available for viewing in the visitors center.

For more information:

Refuge Manager, Montezuma National Wildlife Refuge, 3395 Routes 5 7 20 East, Seneca Falls, NY 13148; 315-568-5987.

LETCHWORTH STATE PARK

Letchworth State Park, south of Buffalo and Rochester, has been dubbed the Grand Canyon of the East. Though Letchworth is much smaller than Arizona's famed canyon and is largely unknown outside New York State, it is still a spectacular gorge.

It is here that the Genesee River runs fast and deep between towering rock walls, forming a seventeen-mile gorge with three major waterfalls. The park is named after nineteenth-century Buffalo industrialist William Pryor Letchworth, who rescued and preserved the area.

The park's creator first spotted the area one day while returning from a trip to New York on the Erie Railway. A newsboy came through the cars with handbills touting the upcoming bridge as "the longest and highest wooden bridge in the United States, if not in the world; and one of the grandest views on the Western continent."

Letchworth was overcome by the scene. A perfect rainbow arched over a waterfall. He saw the beauty despite the timber operations that had scarred the river's banks and all but devastated the area. The industrialist soon set about buying a large house he had seen near the gorge and as much land as he could. Letchworth liked the word "iris," a synonym for rainbow, and named his estate Glen Iris. He continued to buy land in the valley and eventually had 700 acres.

Letchworth retired early from business and devoted himself to social reform. His efforts bettered the lives of thousands of Native Americans, the poor, juvenile delinquents, prisoners, epileptics, the blind, and the mentally ill.

An early and ardent conservationist, Letchworth returned the scarred landscape to a place of unspoiled beauty. Many of the thousands of trees he planted on his estate are still standing today. However, the bridge across the gorge that first attracted Letchworth to the area did not survive a terrible fire, a disaster that saw Letchworth take on the role of police reporter for the *Buffalo Courier*. On May 6, 1875, he reported:

"I was aroused from sleep at ten minutes to four o'clock, and in a few minutes was standing on the lawn at Glen Iris, from which point every portion of the bridge was visible, as well as the Upper Falls, the river and the Middle Falls. The spectacle at precisely four o'clock was fearfully grand; every timber in the bridge seemed then to be ignited, as an open network of fire was stretched across the upper end of the valley . . . the water in the river was glistening with the bright glare thrown on it, and the whole valley of Glen Iris was illuminated with tragic splendor."

The wooden bridge was later replaced with the metal span that still stands in Letchworth Park today.

Letchworth was deeply interested in the history of his land and learned much from local surveyor John Stearns Minard, a student of local history. It was through Minard that he learned of the council house in nearby Caneadea, probably the only building remaining from the days of the Iroquois Confederacy. To preserve the house, Letchworth had it moved to his estate near Middle Falls, where it stands today.

After months of planning, Letchworth conducted the Last Council of the Genesee to rededicate the Council House on October 1, 1872. No such council had been held for seventy years, and none would be held again. He extended invitations to descendants of Indian leaders. Spectators included former President Millard Fillmore and a descendant of the famed Red Jacket.

After the ceremony the Native Americans had a surprise for Letchworth—they wanted to adopt him into the Seneca Nation. He protested at first, but finally agreed. In a solemn ceremony, the Senecas named him Hai-wa-ye-is-ta, "the man who always does the right thing." By initiating him as a blood brother they were giving Letchworth their highest honor.

Letchworth then had the remains of Mary Jemison—the legendary "White Woman of the Genesee"—moved from a cemetery in Buffalo to the council-house grounds. Mary Jemison was born on the high seas in 1743 as her parents were coming from Belfast, Ireland, to America, where they settled in Pennsylvania. When Mary was fifteen, her family was attacked and killed by a Native American war party. Saved and turned over to

Senecas who had lost warriors in the attack on the settlers, she was adopted and given the name "Dehgewanus."

Several times in later years, Mary had the opportunity to return to the settlers' world, but she always refused. As a young bride she walked some 600 miles with her baby on her back, from Ohio to the Genesee Valley. After the American Revolution, during the great Council of 1797 at Big Tree near Genesee, Mary was granted a tract of land known as the Gardeau Tract. It consisted of about 17,000 acres and included some of the property that eventually came into Letchworth's hands.

Mary Jemison lived out her long life as a Seneca in the shadow of the gorge, dying at ninety-one. Letchworth had a statue erected marking Mary Jemison's final resting place. She is depicted with long, braided hair and with her baby strapped to her back as she would have looked during her long trek from the Ohio River Valley.

Close to the Seneca Council House is a cabin that Mary Jemison built for her daughter Nancy. Letchworth had it moved to his land to preserve it.

From the beginning, Letchworth not only shared the beauty of Glen Iris with family, friends, and the public who journeyed by train, but during the summer he also brought children from Buffalo orphanages for two-week stays in the fresh air. He always intended Glen Iris as a place where the public would be welcome. Determined to ensure that future generations would be able to enjoy the land, which now totaled 1,000 acres, he joined the American Scenic and Historic Preservation Society and worked out a plan whereby he would give the state his land and home, and the society would maintain jurisdiction over the park. He would retain life use of the property. On December 31, 1906, Letchworth deeded his land to the state.

Still, all was not safe. A bill had been introduced that would continue the charter of the Genesee River Company to submerge part of the park and divert water from the falls. Letchworth hired an attorney to fight the bill and marshaled the forces of his newspaper editor and publisher friends. They won the battle, and the park was saved forever from the electric company. The only remaining danger was that the state itself would build a dam at Portage, but again Letchworth's arguments carried the day.

Letchworth immediately set to work directing the repair of roads, stairs, paths, and retaining walls. More tables and benches were put up, and shelters were built. After Letchworth's death on December 1, 1910, the state began acquiring more land. Today the park encompasses more than 14,350 acres of magnificent scenery: dramatic cliffs along the Genesee that rise in places to 600 feet; three waterfalls, one of them 107 feet high; lush forests; and miles of hiking trails.

It's often possible to see the rainbow that so enchanted Letchworth just beyond Middle Falls. Although every season has its special charms, most visitors agree that the park is at its best on a fine fall day when the colors are at their peak. Glen Iris, which started life as a simple frame home in the 1820s, is usually booked two years or more in advance for fall weekends. It boasts a wonderful wraparound, pillared porch filled with rocking chairs. Each of the simple but comfortable guest rooms is named after a different variety of tree found in the park. The Birch and Cherry rooms have views of the falls.

The history of the lands and Letchworth himself is told in a slide show, artifacts, books, and displays in the William Pryor Letchworth Museum, across the parking lot from the Glen Iris Inn. Although it opened in 1913, three years after his death, the museum had been planned by Letchworth to expand his original Genesee Valley Museum.

Millions of years of geological history are evident in the rock formations throughout the park, where shale and sandstone formed during the Devonian period under the shallow interior seas. Tens of millions of years of erosion wore away great depths of rock, forming river valleys. Glaciers deposited large masses

A QUIET RIDE

For an extraordinary view of Letchworth Park, the gorge, the train trestle, and the park's wildlife, take a ride over the park and surrounding countryside with Balloons Over Letchworth.

There is a magical, other-worldly quality to flying in a hot-air balloon—the world's first form of aviation. The first sensation is one of quiet—intense quiet broken from time to time by the firing of the propane burners. Because the balloons are so quiet, they don't disturb wildlife. It's commonplace to see whitetail deer loping along, seemingly taking you on a tour of their park.

You won't feel any wind, because you are actually floating in the wind. The balloons go up only when weather conditions are ideal during the early morning or early evening, when the winds are the lightest.

Seven stories high and made of 1,200 yards of nylon, the balloons float quietly over the falls, the river, and the train trestle. In the French tradition, each flight ends with champagne. The champagne tradition developed as a way to calm French farmers who were upset when balloons landed in their fields.

Morning flights from May 1 to August 30 include breakfast at the Glen Iris Inn. The balloon is launched at the Middle/Upper Falls picnic area, 1,000 feet south of the Glen Iris Inn. For more information or reservations, contact Balloons Over Letchworth, 85 North Cavalier Road, Scottsville, NY 14546; 716-889-8070. The cost is $185 for one or $350 per couple. The off-season rate, from November 15 to April 15, is $300 for two.

of material blocking the original valleys. The seventeen miles of winding, deep canyons and valleys of the Genesee Gorge are a product of glacial blocking of an early river bed. Each year the river cuts deeper into the dramatic cliffs, some of which are already 600 feet high.

Nearly every species of North American tree grows here, thanks to Letchworth. There is also a good variety of wildflowers, including several species of orchid, which are all protected and should not be picked or harmed. You are likely to see woodchucks and deer along the road at twilight. Raccoons abound; they can be a nuisance and should be avoided. Rabies has been found in raccoons in this area. Park rules and common sense should deter you from feeding these animals, often called bandits because of the masks across their eyes and their penchant for stealing goodies, especially food from campers. The 270 campsites are open May 15 to October 15 and cost $12.00 per night. The Trailside Lodge Winter Recreation Area offers cross-country skiing, snowmobiling, skating, and tubing. Guided nature walks are available throughout the year. Hunting is allowed during the fall, with special permits.

There's a gift shop in the Glen Iris Inn and a campstore in the park. Information and park literature is available at the William Pryor Letchworth Museum, as are exhibits on Letchworth, the park, Native Americans, Mary Jemison, and the life of pioneers in the Genesee Valley.

Where: The park is 50 miles southeast of Buffalo and 35 miles south of Rochester. Take US 20A south of East Aurora to State 39 south for the northern Perry entrance, or farther east to State 36 south for the Mount Morris entrance. Or continue on State 39 south through Castile to reach the Castile entrance, which is the only one open in winter.

Hours: 6 A.M. to 10 P.M., except assigned rented sites.

Admission: $3.00 per car Memorial Day to Labor Day; free in off-season.

Best time to visit: It's hard to match Letchworth on a fine fall day. Summer is the time when all the facilities of the park, including the two swimming pools, are open.

Activities: Camping, guided walks, hiking, workshops, guided ski treks, winter recreation, fishing, swimming, hunting, raft trips.

Concessions: In addition to the Glen Iris Inn, there are two restaurants and several snack bars throughout the park. Adventure Calls, 20 Ellicott Avenue, Batavia, NY 14020, operates raft trips in the gorge during the spring, summer, and fall as long as water levels are adequate. The trips operate on weekends and holidays and during the summer also on Mondays and Fridays. The cost is $20.00 on weekdays and $23.00 on weekends. Wetsuit rentals are available during the cooler weather. Call 716-343-4710 for information and reservations.

Pets: Household pets are allowed on a leash. Proof of a current rabies certificate is required.

For more information:

Letchworth State Park, 1 Letchworth State Park, Castile, NY 14427; 716-493-2611.

Campsite reservations, 800-456-CAMP.

SONNENBERG GARDENS

A great bronze Buddha sits in the lotus position in the Japanese Garden, an oasis of serenity under sheltering trees and one of the ten formal gardens at Sonnenberg Gardens. Sonnenberg, meaning "sunny hill" in German, is a magnificent, fifty-acre, turn-of-the-century garden estate in Canandaigua, just a few minutes north of Canandaigua Lake. The Smithsonian Institution has recognized Sonnenberg as "one of the most magnificent late Victorian gardens ever created in America."

This was the summer home of Frederick Ferris Thompson and his wife, Mary Clark Thompson, of New York City. The home, completed in 1887, is a handsome forty-room mansion of gray stone trimmed with reddish Medina sandstone. From the mansion the deep blue waters of Canandaigua Lake can be seen between the trees.

After her husband's death Mrs. Thompson took an extensive world tour and became inspired by the many spectacular gardens she visited. Soon after she returned home she commissioned Ernest W. Bowdich, a noted Boston horticulturist and landscape gardener, to design and supervise the construction of gardens at Sonnenberg as a memorial to her husband. The Japanese Garden, surely one of the most beautiful, was designed and built by K. Wadamori, a noted Japanese artist, who brought six assistants with him from Japan to work on the project. The gardens were constructed over an eighteen-year period.

Until Mrs. Thompson's death in 1923, many distinguished guests were entertained at Sonnenberg, and each was invited to plant a rare tree to commemorate his or her visit. Many of the trees have grown into magnificent specimens that add great beauty to the grounds. As soon as the gardens were completed, they were opened to the public from time to time, and as many as 7,000 people would come on a visitors' day.

After the owner's death, her nephew sold Sonnenberg to the federal government in 1931. A Veterans Administration hospital was built on part of the grounds, with the mansion serving as a nurses' dormitory. The gardens and grounds were neglected but never destroyed. In 1973, the home and gardens was deeded to Sonnenberg Gardens, a not-for-profit corporation created to restore the gardens and mansion to their former glory.

The Rose Garden was the first to be restored. Volunteers planted more than 4,000 bushes, which are particularly glorious in June when every bush is a blaze of color.

The Japanese Garden is considered the real gem of Sonnenberg. In 1916 the late Willam T. Hornaday, then director of the New York Zoological Gardens, said of the Japanese Garden: "Every sweep of the eye embraces a gemlike lily pool or a brook; rocks that look as if they grew there, stone jewels of garden architecture and statues that fit their surroundings." There is a pair of stone devil dogs, one smiling to welcome friends, the other scowling to ward off evil spirits. The waterways are spanned by small bridges. There's even a teahouse based on one in Kyoto, Japan.

Among the other gardens are the Rock, Old Fashioned, Pansy, Moonlight, and Secret Gardens, the last planned for quiet moments of contemplation. The Moonlight Garden is predominantly white and is arranged so that its blossoms are illuminated by the moon.

The Rock Garden is composed of pudding stone and Onondaga limestone, two conglomerate rocks selected for their natural indentations and pockets—perfect homes for rock plants. Geysers and simulated springs shoot up. A statue of the mythological creature Pan with his human body and goat's legs, horns, and ears adds the proper touch to this garden.

The Sonnenberg Mansion is on the National Register of Historic Places and has been beautifully restored. Free tours of the gardens are offered daily, or you may stroll on your own. Staff is on duty inside the mansion, but there is no guided tour of the house; descriptions are posted throughout. The medieval Great Hall is decorated with an elk head and a minstrel gallery. Mary Clark Thompson's favorite room was the library. The axis of the Italian garden is framed through the French doors of the library.

Where: Take the New York Thruway (I-90) west to exit 43 onto State 21 into Canandaigua, where it becomes Gibson Street, and follow the signs. From the Thruway heading east, take exit 44 onto State 332 into Canandaigua, where it becomes Main Street; take a left onto Gibson Street and follow the signs.

Hours: 9:30 A.M. to 5:30 P.M. daily from mid-May to mid-October. Guided tours at 10:00 A.M. and 2:00 P.M., or you may stroll on your own anytime during open hours. From late November through January 1, there's a Festival of Lights from 4:30 P.M. to 9:30 P.M.

Admission: $6.00 for adults; $5.00 for seniors 55 and over; $2.00 for children 6 to 16, and free under 6. During the Festival of Lights, admission is $5.00 for adults and $3.00 for children, including wagon rides, or $1.50 for adults and fifty cents for children for mansion admission.

Best time to visit: Anytime during the growing season.

Activities: Garden lectures and tours, Antique Rose week in June, concerts, Teddy Bear Picnic.

Concessions: Gift shop, restaurant, Canandaigua Wine Tasting Room, horse-drawn-wagon rides during the Festival of Lights.

Pets: Not allowed.

For more information:

Sonnenberg Gardens and Mansion, 151 Charlotte Street, Canandaigua, NY 14424; 716-924-5420.

CUMMING NATURE CENTER OF THE ROCHESTER MUSEUM & SCIENCE CENTER

How many pancakes covered in fresh maple syrup do hungry visitors consume during Maple Sugaring Days at the Rochester Museum & Science Center's Cumming Nature Center?

No one has kept a precise count, but the event, which runs for three weekends, has grown in popularity since its beginnings in 1976. Each year, more than 250 taps are inserted into maple trees in late February, when lengthening days and slightly warmer temperatures trigger the flow of sap. The event is a spring highlight at the 900-acre living museum in Naples, south of Rochester. Demonstrations are given to show how the sap is boiled down to transform the trees' sap into one of nature's finest taste treats.

The nature center was donated in 1972 by Mr. and Mrs. Howard Cumming to the Rochester Museum & Science Center. It has been designated a national environmental study area by the National Park Service. Six miles of thematic trails lead visitors through forests, wetlands, and plantations.

Visitors learn how prehistoric Iroquois and pioneering

settlers treated their environments. All trails begin at the visitors center, which serves as a reception area featuring multimedia theater presentations, wildlife art exhibits, and environment-related displays. The building also houses a snack bar, a gift shop, restrooms, a cross-country ski and snowshoe rental area, and homes for animals used in the Wildlife of New York education program, including birds, mammals, and reptiles.

The Beaver Trail takes visitors to an observation tower overlooking a thirty-five-acre beaver pond. Forest management practiced by the center is interpreted as you follow the Conservation Trail to the operational sawmill.

The Helen Gordon Trail is a unique outdoor art gallery with paintings by ecologist and artist Jerry Czech to acquaint you with the birds and animals of the area. The Iroquois Trail provides a visual history of the Six Nations through the paintings of Seneca artist Ernest Smith. The Pioneer Trail's reconstructed eighteenth-century homestead offers an informative walk into the past, complete with a resident yoke of oxen.

Every weekend, live bird-of-prey shows are presented, featuring a majestic red-tailed hawk. School programs bring thousands of children to the center each year. Year-round classes are offered in ecology, natural science, art, and pioneer life. Skis and snowshoes can be rented here.

Where: Gulick Road, Naples—south of Honeoye. From the east: State 5/US 20 to US 20A, left onto US 20A/State 64, right onto 20A to East Lake Road to Honeoye, left onto East Lake Road, then follow the Nature Center signs. From the west: I-390 south to State 5/US 20, east on 5/20 to State 15A in Lima, right onto 15A to 20A in Hemlock, left onto 20A to East Lake Road in Honeoye, right onto East Lake Road, then follow the Nature Center signs. From the south: Route 17 to I-390N to Concocton, State 371 to State 21 to Clark Street in Naples. Left onto Clark Street to Gulick Road to the Nature Center.

Hours: 9:00 A.M. to 5:00 P.M., Wednesday through Sunday. Closed November 14 to December 28.

Admission: $4.00 for adults and $1.50 for kindergarteners through twelfth graders; preschoolers are free.

Best time to visit: During the maple-sugar weekends if you are a maple-syrup lover. If snow conditions are right you can combine cross-country skiing with eating pancakes and maple syrup. The beautiful fall season is celebrated with Fall Harvest Days. There are workshops and the opportunity to follow a tree from log to board.

Pets: Not allowed.

Activities: Maple Sugaring Days, living museum, nature walks, bird-of-prey shows, cross-country skiing, Fall Harvest Days.

For more information:

RMSC Cumming Nature Center, 6472 Gulick Road, Naples, NY 14012; 716-374-6160.

4

Adirondacks

*Few fully understand what the Adirondack wilderness really is.
It is a mystery even to those who have crossed and
recrossed it by boats along its avenues—the lakes; and on
foot through its vast and silent recesses. Though the woodman
may pass his lifetime in some section of the wilderness,
it is still a mystery to him.*

—Verplanck Colvin

ADIRONDACK PARK

Adirondack Park is big. That's something of an understatement.
The park is bigger than Yellowstone, Yosemite, and Glacier
National Parks combined.

This state park in northern New York is unique in many
ways. You don't have to pay an entry fee when you cross the
park's boundaries, known as the Blue Line since the first maps
of the park more than a century ago showed the area delineated
in blue.

And people live here, making the area far more diverse than any federal park. This human history has become part of the history of the United States. About the size of the state of Vermont, Adirondack Park is genuine wilderness that is easily accessible to a large population within the United States and nearby Canada.

But the lack of an entrance gate, the sheer size, and the towns within the park can be confusing. People sometimes drive right through without even realizing they've been in the largest park in the lower forty-eight states. There is a subtlety about the park, a quality of unexpectedness. Instead of civilization outside and wilderness inside, there's a unique mixture here.

Established in 1892, Adirondack Park covers 6.1 million acres of public and private land, or much of the northern third of New York State. It includes the Adirondack Forest Preserve, established in 1885 as the forty-two percent of the park that is public land, forever wild and preserved as wilderness.

In 1894, the New York State Constitution was amended to state: "The lands of the state, now owned or hereafter acquired, constituting the forest preserve as now fixed by law shall be forever kept as wild forest lands." This "forever wild" concept now appears in Article XIV, Section I of the state constitution; it has long been the rallying cry of New York State's conservationists.

The Adirondack Mountains occupy the northeast quarter of the park. Some of the approximately 100 peaks are on private land; forty-plus are more than 4,000 feet above sea level. The mountains were rounded off and smoothed down by the weight of glacial ice during the last Ice Age. Geologists now suspect that the range is still growing three times faster than the Alps. Still, they're growing at a rate of only three millimeters every forty-four years. Within the range are 2,200 glacier-formed ponds and lakes and 30,000 miles of rivers and streams.

This is an ideal area for climbing, hiking, hunting, camping, canoeing, fishing, swimming, cycling, skiing, and just plain enjoying the clean mountain air.

The Adirondacks have long had an image problem. In 1792 the region was described as "waste and unappropriated." The name *Adirondacks* came about through an expedition organized by a Williams College professor, Ebenezer Emmons, who led the state's first Natural History Survey in 1837. He christened Mount Marcy after the sitting New York governor. Emmons wrote: "I propose to call the mountains the Adirondack Group, a name by which a well-known tribe of Indians who once hunted here may be commemorated."

So much for good intentions. Emmons was thinking of the Huron word meaning "they of the Rock Clan," but the word is actually an Iroquois term of insult meaning "bark eaters," used to imply that someone was such a poor hunter that he was reduced to eating tree bark. (The upstate tribes used the North Woods for hunting but spent the winters in the more temperate lowlands.)

William Verner, former Adirondack Museum curator, described the Adirondacks as "a huge wilderness island poking impudently above the highly civilized sea of the northeast."

The interior of the park remained silent in its splendor until after the Civil War, when a tourist boom began. Inspired by the Reverend William Henry Harrison Murray's *Adventures in the Wilderness or Camp Life in the Adirondacks,* published in 1869, tourists stampeded northward. The region was forever changed. An entire industry grew up, spawning inns with guides who took the "city sports" hunting and fishing. The building of more and more lavish hotels followed, along with better transportation.

The Adirondack region became one of the major playgrounds for the rich and famous of that gilded age in American history between the end of the Civil War and the beginning of World War I.

The healthful effects of the clean mountain air attracted many, including tuberculosis patients. Dr. Edward L. Trudeau

Moose browse for water plants along the lake edge

founded the Trudeau Institute on Saranac Lake in 1885, bringing national attention to the pristine lake and tiny village. Patients from near and far came seeking a cure, among them Robert Louis Stevenson, who came in a futile attempt to regain his health. He began *The Master of Ballantrae* during his stay. Stevenson once called the Adirondacks "Little Switzerland," but other writings seem to reveal his true feelings. Describing his Adirondack winter, during which he slept on an unheated porch, he wrote: "The mercury in the thermometer curls into the bulb like a hibernating bear." He also wrote that "the grayness of the heavens here is a circumstance eminently revolting to the soul."

TEDDY ROOSEVELT

In September 1901, Vice President Theodore Roosevelt brought worldwide attention to the region that Roosevelt called "the most remote human habitation in the Empire State." Leaving President William McKinley recovering from an assassin's bullet in Buffalo, Roosevelt came to the Adirondacks, where his family was waiting. The group arranged for a guide to take them to Mount Marcy, at 5,344 feet the highest peak in the state.

While Roosevelt was lunching at Lake Tear-of-the-Clouds, a messenger arrived to notify the vice president that McKinley had taken a turn for the worse. Needing to rush back to Buffalo, Roosevelt proceeded to take a ride down the mountain that was headlined in newspapers around the world.

It wasn't until he reached North Creek station that the vice president learned the terrible truth—the president had died. A historic marker between Minerva and Newcomb commemorates the estimated point where Roosevelt became president.

As a youngster, frail and suffering from poor health, Teddy Roosevelt spent three happy summers at Paul Smith's Hotel on St. Regis Lake. It is not too farfetched to say that the Adirondacks shaped Roosevelt's personal passion for nature.

As an adult, Roosevelt traveled the world but returned often to the Adirondacks. It is fitting that it was during a visit to this mountain wilderness that his life was to change forever. The man who became president in the wilds of New York's largest wilderness preserve (although he actually took the oath of office in Buffalo) championed the cause of conservation throughout his life.

A prolific writer, Roosevelt wrote often of the wilderness, of camping, and of hunting: "There are no words that can tell the hidden spirit of the wilderness, that can reveal its mystery, its melancholy, and its charms.

"I recognize the right and duty of this generation to develop and use the natural resources of our land; but I do not recognize the right to waste them, or to rob, by wasteful use, the generations that come after us."

While president and against powerful opposition, Roosevelt set aside 150 million acres of forest and created more than fifty game preserves and sixteen national monuments, the best known of which is the Grand Canyon.

OTHER PRESIDENTIAL VISITS

There's no report of George Washington sleeping in the Adirondacks. However, Thomas Jefferson and James Madison visited Lake George in 1791 on a combination reconnaissance of Vermont and vacation. Jefferson, a world traveler, described the lake as the most beautiful he had ever seen.

In 1817, James Monroe skirted the edge of what would become the park in a trip from Champlain to Sackets Harbor on the St. Lawrence River. Andrew Jackson, aka Old Hickory, was a close friend of Richard Keese II, after whom the village of Keeseville is named. When Jackson visited Keese, a tree was planted in honor of the occasion. Alas, no hickories could be found, so a walnut was substituted.

Chester A. Arthur stayed at Mart Moody's Mount Morrie House near Tupper Lake and slept on the floor like everyone else. When he was president, Arthur named guide and innkeeper Moody to the job of postmaster for the settlement of Moody.

Grover Cleveland also knew Mart Moody as a guide. While hunting near Big Wolf Pond he told Moody, "There's no wolves here, darn it! But there ain't a hundred pencils here, either, goin' every minute to take down everything I say." Cleveland returned to the Adirondacks for his honeymoon, staying at posh places on Lake Placid and Saranac Lake.

President Benjamin Harrison campaigned in Loon Lake and other communities before the 1892 election. In 1895 Harrison built a rustic log camp on Second Lake near Old Forge.

William McKinley visited John Brown's grave near Lake Placid in 1897. Unfortunately, it is McKinley's assassination, not that visit, that links the twenty-fifth president and the Adirondacks most closely. Vice President Theodore Roosevelt, vacationing in the mountains when McKinley died, had to rush down the mountain at a record-setting pace to take the oath of office.

Calvin Coolidge established a summer White House at White Pine Camp on Osgood Pond in 1926. Franklin D. Roosevelt officiated at the opening of the 1932 Winter Olympics in Lake Placid, dedicated the Whiteface Memorial Highway in 1935, and celebrated the fiftieth anniversary of the forest preserve in Lake Placid the same year.

After his winter stay the writer left for the warmer climes of the South Pacific and never returned. His cottage has been preserved as a shrine and is open to the public.

Sigmund Freud had a considerably warmer memory of the Adirondacks than Stevenson, writing a friend back in Vienna: "Of all things that I have experienced in America, this is by far the most amazing. Everything is left very rough and primitive but it comes off. Mixing bowls serve as wash bowls, china mugs for glasses, etc. We took trails and came down slopes to which even my horns and hoofs were not equal."

In 1893, Baedeker's *United States* described the region as the "Adirondack Wilderness, densely covered with forest, much of it still virgin and almost unexplored."

ADIRONDACK MUSEUM

One of the best introductions to the Adirondacks is the Adirondack Museum in the pristine village of Blue Mountain Lake. The museum is nationally acclaimed for its exhibits on life, work, and leisure in the Adirondack region.

Rated as one of the finest regional museums in the country, the institution aims to chronicle the entire Adirondack experience.

A driving force behind the museum was Harold K. Hochschild, who had been coming to Blue Mountain Lake with his family since the turn of the century. The result of the Hochschild family involvement is a well-endowed enclave that entertains and educates. After several years of work and forays into the park to collect wagons, boats, and other remnants of the region's heritage, the museum opened on August 3, 1957. Since then, several million visitors have explored the twenty-two separate exhibit buildings spread over a thirty-acre compound on a peninsula nearly surrounded by the lake.

Begin at the main building with its exhibits highlighting the land and history of the region. A large push-button map allows visitors to illuminate towns, rivers, mountains, and lakes throughout the park.

Detailed dioramas are accompanied by "hearphones," head-sets that provide explanations of the scenes before you. You'll be amazed at a model of the loggers' cookhouse, where nineteenth-century lumberjacks consumed prodigious meals. At one camp, we are told, the crew of forty loggers were known to have con-sumed 400 eggs, three whole hams, and countless loaves of bread in a single sitting.

Visit a log hotel built in 1876 and see what visitors to the Adirondacks enjoyed in the nineteenth century. Writing in 1873, one visitor observed "games of croquet on the lawn, boating parties upon the lake, lovers sauntering in the woods, and a Chickering thrumming in the parlor."

"Woods and Waters: Outdoor Recreation in the Adiron-dacks," another exhibit building, could be a museum in its own right. When you enter the building, you'll pass through simulated outdoor settings—following a trail into the woods, walking across a stream on a rustic bridge. There's a simple lean-to with a campfire blazing, birds chirping, a canoe pulled up on the shore. In an old hermit's cabin you can hear an actual radio inter-view with the cabin's one-time occupant, Noah John Rondeau.

One building contains nothing but boats—Adirondack guide boats, sail canoes, polished teak speedboats, a naphtha-fueled launch that looks like a truncated steamboat, a Colonial-era bateau.

Another building is given over to stagecoaches, buckboard wagons, carriages, and horse-drawn sleighs, one with a fox-fur lap robe that E.H. Harrison gave to tuberculosis pioneer Dr. Edward Trudeau.

An almost elegant two-seater outhouse is on display, and there's an exhibit on the infamous blackflies of June and the mosquitoes and deerflies of midsummer. Logging and mining exhibits portray the industries that proved both vital and devastating to the region.

The boat pond contains vessels dating from early in this century, including the steamboat *Osprey* and the excursion launch *Mountaineer*. Displays on trapping include the pelts of otter, bobcat, bear, and other animals, along with traps, early snowshoes, and eight wooden toboggans and sleds. There's an 1890 hearse with wheels for summer and runners for winter.

If you admire fine craftsmanship, you'll marvel over the 800 wooden miniatures made by one local man—everything from an elegant circus wagon to 407 chairs, no two the same.

A long photo belt allows you to take a seat and watch historic photographs pass by. The photos give visitors a sense of the people who were drawn to the Adirondacks and the lives they led.

The Adirondack Museum Library is open weekdays throughout the year to researchers who make arrangements with the museum's librarian prior to a visit. The book collection includes more than 8,000 published volumes on the Adirondacks, New York history, environmental issues, and outdoor recreation. The library owns nearly 600 linear feet of manuscript material produced by individuals, businesses, institutions, and organizations. The museum also owns a large collection of maps, journals, and magazines.

The museum store sells books and prints of Adirondack paintings, posters, and photos. They are also available through mail order.

Where: One mile north of the village of Blue Mountain Lake on State 30.

Hours: 9:30 A.M. to 5:30 P.M. daily from Memorial Day weekend through mid-October. Admission closes at 4:30 P.M.

Admission: $10.00 adults, $9.00 seniors, $6.00 children.

Best time to visit: Anytime. A museum visit can be a good rainy-day activity.

Concessions: Cafeteria and gift shop.
Pets: Not allowed, except for guide dogs.
For more information:
     The Adirondack Museum, Blue Mountain Lake, NY 12812;
518-352-7311.

SAGAMORE INSTITUTE

Today it's a simple drive to the Sagamore on the shore of Saga-more Lake in the center of the Adirondacks. When the century was young, it was a real journey to this Great Camp. Guests came by a relay of motor launch and private train, chugging along the half mile that made up the shortest track in the country to join the party at Alfred Vanderbilt's summer retreat.

     Houseguests included Gary Cooper, Eddy Duchin, Jean Arthur, and Madame Chiang Kai-shek. "I like every game there is," Vanderbilt's second wife, Margaret Emerson, announced. "We must play fifty a day." And what a time they had.

     William West Durant first hit on the idea and design for the Great Camps of the Adirondacks. Actually the word "camp" is a masterpiece of understatement for these millionaires' comfortable compounds in the woods.

     After developing his skills on Camp Pine Knot for Collis P. Huntington and Uncas for J. P. Morgan, Durant constructed Sagamore, which Alfred Vanderbilt bought in 1901 for $160,000. The massive main lodge was built along the lines of a Swiss music box. Even though Vanderbilt spent most of his time else-where, Sagamore was a self-contained village in the heart of the wilderness with its own farm. There were twenty-nine structures grouped into a family and guest complex on a wooded promon-tory on Sagamore Lake and a servant and service area a quarter of a mile away.

     Inside the cedarbark-sided cottages were Renoirs and

Remingtons and twenty-six stone fireplaces. A large support staff of carpenters, ironworkers, cooks, and guides kept this village humming. Cooks packed cold picnics of squab and filet mignon so the guests could "rough it."

A national historic site, the camp now is operated by the nonprofit Sagamore Institute. Sagamore offers a perfect introduction to the Adirondacks and the outdoors.

Don't expect Gilded Age luxury service. The staff is now greatly reduced, and menus are simple but wholesome. The Sagamore doesn't have a liquor license, but guests are welcome to bring their own wine or other liquor.

Sagamore's buildings are maintained much as they were at the turn of the century. There are no locks on the doors, few phones, and no television. The bowling alley dating back to 1914 has been refinished recently. It is semi-outdoor and unique to Great Camp architecture.

The Sagamore is open year-round (except for April), and almost every weekend is devoted to outdoor education and nature programs for families and people of all ages and interests. During the winter, cross-country skiing is popular. Spend the day with one of the New York State guides on the old carriage and logging roads that run through the adjacent forest preserve. Or go out with a naturalist on snowshoes for a wildlife tracking class.

Spring is a celebration of the forest's awakening, with a focus on birding, wildflowers, and strategies for dealing with the region's infamous insects. During July and August the focus switches to paddles and pathways. Navigate the cedar-studded shores of Sagamore Lake, hike on the trails, or climb the mountains that surround the Sagamore.

Autumn weekends offer unparalleled leaf-peeping opportunities, traditional crafts, hiking, and the enjoyment of the change of seasons. After sunset, the Great Camps history programs begin. The programs feature guest speakers discussing wildlife

The wake-robin or trillium blooms in the woods

topics or musicians filling the camp with folk or mountain music. You may thrill to a loon calling across the lake or the dazzling spectacle of the northern lights.

A variety of special programs throughout the year includes fly-fishing, mountain biking, kayaking, llama trekking, rock climbing, women in the wilderness, woodcarving, photography, papermaking, basketry, rustic furniture, and flytying. Special holiday celebrations feature storytelling, mountain music and dance, and mountain dulcimers. Two-hour history tours begin at 10:00 A.M. and 1:30 P.M. daily from July 4 to Labor Day and weekends-only from Labor Day to Columbus Day. These are ideal for day visitors.

Whatever your interest, the Sagamore offers a good mix of entertainment, education, and free time, plus the chance to experience a special Adirondack Great Camp. And you don't even need to be a friend of the Vanderbilts to do it.

Elderhostel programs are held at Sagamore throughout the year. One of the institute's most popular and unique programs is the Grandparents' and Grandchildren's Summer Camp held during three one-week periods in the summer. The program was designed by the Foundation for Grandparenting and provides activities for grandparents and grandchildren together and separately.

Where: State 28 to Raquette Lake. Turn right at the school and follow the dirt road four miles to Sagamore.

Hours: All day, year-round, except for April, when the Sagamore is closed for mud season. Some weekends are closed to the public because of private parties, weddings, or reunions.

Admission: Varies with program and length of visit. The cost of the tour is $6.00, $3.00 for children.

Best time to visit: Summers are popular with everyone. It's hard to beat a perfect fall weekend, and winter and spring have their special charms. Most visitors try to avoid the black-fly season in late May and June.

Activities: History tours for day users and a variety of residential programs that offer education, entertainment, and nature study. Tuition includes three meals a day, double rooms, and the use of swimming areas and canoes. Guests are invited to bring bowling balls. Tuition also includes the workshop of your choice.

Concessions: The snack shop is open for refreshments and light lunches. The Sagamore Store offers authentic crafts, souvenirs, and book titles pertinent to the area.

Pets: Not permitted.
For more information:
    Sagamore, PO Box 146, Raquette Lake, NY 13436; 315-354-5311.

LAKE GEORGE, THE SOUTHERN ADIRONDACKS, AND LAKE CHAMPLAIN VALLEY

For the purpose of exploring, we will divide Adirondack Park into four regions: Lake George, the Southern Adirondacks, and Lake Champlain Valley; the High Peaks and Northern Adirondacks; the Northwest Lakes Region; and the Central and Southwestern Adirondacks.

Many Adirondack devotees quickly develop a love of a particular area and return again and again. This is especially true if visits begin in childhood.

I must confess a particular fondness for Blue Mountain Lake in the heart of the park. To me and many others, Blue Mountain possesses the absolute essence of the park, representing the perfect Adirondack lake, mountain, and village. Perfectly beautiful, it is a jewel in the treasure chest that is Adirondack Park.

However, there are many other jewels here for lovers of the outdoors or anyone who wishes a unique wilderness experience.

Lake George, at the southeastern boundary of the park, remains a study in contradictions. Thomas Jefferson, an early visitor and world traveler, called Lake George the most beautiful water he had ever seen. Rugged, pine-covered mountains encircle the forty-four-square-mile lake, and hundreds of small islands pepper the deep, dark-blue waters.

Known as the Queen of America's Lakes, Lake George is the perfect gateway to the Adirondacks. It's possible to have a real taste of the wilderness here. On the other hand, the village of Lake George has a 1950s touristy air to it. There's a summer boardwalk atmosphere and plenty of cotton candy and T-shirt shops. Horse-drawn buggies provide rides around town.

Lake George has long been recognized for its strategic importance. In 1755 the English built Fort William Henry on a promontory overlooking the southern end of the lake to block any French advance from Canada into the colonies along the Lake Champlain–Hudson River Valley route.

James Fenimore Cooper used the tragedy of Fort William Henry as the central theme for his classic *The Last of the Mohicans* as a tribute to the men, women, and children who died there when the French attacked. For six days and nights in 1757 the French mercilessly pounded the log fort. Finally, the British surrendered, the fort was burned, and hundreds were slaughtered.

A highlight of the tour of the fort includes demonstrations of musket firing. There are many guides at this site in eighteenth-century dress, and their uniforms are quite spectacular. The fort looks down the length of Lake George, and the view alone is worth the stop.

The Lake George Steamboat Cruise Company, which claims to be the oldest boat-excursion company in the country, has been offering passenger rides since 1817. Four cruise boats travel the length of Lake George on one- to four-hour excursions. The steamboats provide a good overview of the lake, its history, and attractions.

Lake George has long been known as one of the big fishbowls of the Northeast. On a recent fishing excursion with Bigfoot Charters, we caught four nice-sized lake trout in a few hours.

The Adirondack Trout Fishing Preserve offers an easy introduction to fishing. The preserve is stocked with brook, rainbow, and golden rainbow trout. It's the perfect place for children. No fishing license is required, and you don't even have to bring your own equipment. Rod rentals are available.

Where: US 9, Lake George. At the intersection of US 9 and I-87, exit 21, go a quarter-mile north.

Hours: 10:00 A.M. to 5:00 P.M. daily during July and August.

Admission: Free, but there is a rod-rental charge.

Best time to visit: Anytime.

Concessions: Snack stand.

Activities: Fishing and picnicking.

Pets: Not allowed.

For more information:

Adirondack Trout Fishing Preserve, US 9, Lake George, NY 12845; 518-668-3064.

Adirondack lakes aren't known for their beaches, but Lake George has a well-earned reputation for its superb beaches along the southern end of the lake. Million Dollar Beach, on Beach Road, got its name because of the cost of construction and the ritzy clientele of the resort's early days. It is at the head of Lake George. Other public beaches include Lake Avenue Beach (Lake Avenue, off Beach Road) and Shepard Park (off Canada Street). Lake George Battlefield Park and Public Campground, located directly behind Million Dollar Beach, is a thirty-five-acre park that includes the remains of an old fort as well as monuments to the men who fought there during the French and Indian Wars and the Revolution. Rest rooms, picnic tables, barbecue pits, and overnight campsites are available.

Accommodations in the Lake George area run the gamut from simple campgrounds, RV campgrounds, 1950s-style motels, housekeeping cottages, and bed and breakfasts to the historic and elegant Sagamore Hotel on its own island at Bolton Landing. Opened in 1883, the hotel is listed on the National Register of Historic Places. After a $72 million restoration, the hotel is truly a world-class resort.

If you have a boat or decide to rent one at one of the

marinas in town, you will have access to several island campgrounds operated by the New York State Department of Environmental Conservation. The campgrounds are on islands in Lake George – Glen Island, Narrow Island, and Long Island. There is a delicious feeling to camping on an island. Although you probably won't have the island all to yourself, there is still an aura of separateness to the island camping experience. You will feel worlds away from civilization, although you will be only a boat ride or canoe ride away. If you travel by canoe, it's easy to imagine yourself back in the nineteenth century, when early tourists were discovering the joys of the wilderness experience.

Hiking is popular in the Lake George area, and the Adirondack Mountain Club (Luzerne Road, Lake George, 518-668-4447) hosts frequent weekend and one- and two-day hiking trips throughout the year. Call for a schedule. The club also publishes Adirondack trail guides. State-licensed guides also offer their services for wilderness hiking and rock climbing.

The entrance for the trailhead of Prospect Mountain is in Lake George Village on Montcalm Street. It's a moderate climb to the 2,000-foot summit.

On a clear day you'll be rewarded with spectacular views of the Adirondack High Peaks, the Green Mountains in Vermont, and the White Mountains in New Hampshire.

For a unique view of the lakes and mountains, try a hot-air-balloon ride from nearby Glens Falls. Rides are offered at sunrise and sunset, weather permitting. Every September the Adirondack Balloon Festival is held in nearby Queensbury.

Heading north from Lake George, the next stop, especially if you are a history buff, is Fort Ticonderoga. Built by the French in 1755, the fort was designed to take control of the southern extreme of Lake Champlain and the entire water route between Montreal and Albany. Fort Ticonderoga has been nicknamed "Key to a Continent," an apt description considering its history.

The fort was attacked six times. Three times it was held, and three times it fell – a record no other fort on the continent can approach. Famous figures such as George Washington, Benjamin Franklin, Ethan Allen, the Marquis de Montcalm, and Benedict Arnold walked on these parade grounds. Ethan Allen and his Green Mountain Boys took the fort from the British "in the name of Jehovah and the great Continental Congress." You can wander through the fort independently or join one of the guided tours offered regularly throughout the day. Fife and drum music is performed on the parade ground at regular intervals, and a cannon shoot is also held several times day. On selected weekends there are encampments of regiments reenacting battles. A boat tour is available every day in July and August.

If the day is clear, take a drive up Mount Defiance, once called Rattlesnake Mountain by the French. The Americans called it Sugar Loaf Hill and believed it couldn't be scaled. But British Gen. John Burgoyne proved otherwise, observing, "Where a goat can go a man can go, and where a man can go he can drag a gun."

From the summit of Mount Defiance, General Burgoyne forced the Americans to flee Fort Ticonderoga. Today a steep, narrow, paved road leads to the top. There are a couple of cannon at the top, as if to prove the history of this mountain, but the real draw is the view.

Heading north, you will come to the Ausable Chasm in the northeastern corner of the park. The Ausable River has carved a most impressive path here through deep layers of sandstone, leaving cliffs that reach well over 100 feet high in places. The chasm was formed about five million years ago, when this part of the country was submerged beneath a prehistoric sea. Major John Howe, who discovered the chasm, made his descent suspended on ropes. Today's visitors travel on foot, following stone steps up and down and crossing steel bridges that span the gorge high above the river. The chasm has been operated as a public attraction since 1870.

The walk through the chasm is about three-quarters of a mile long and includes about 150 steps; it takes about half an hour. The walkways can be slippery. You will end up at Table Rock, a platform extending over the river. From here, you'll travel by boat. On crowded summer days be prepared for a wait. Step into one of the oversized red wooden dories. Pull up the green plastic flaps attached to the sides for protection against the foamy waters ahead.

The boats, with two guides in each, are pulled back upstream on cables. The highlight of the ten-minute journey is a bouncing ride through the rapids into the Whirlpool Basin. The trip appeals to all ages. When the boat ride is over, a bus will take you back to the main souvenir shop.

Nature seems far away in the gaudy gift shop where you buy your ticket. One of the biggest shops in the Adirondacks, it includes a cafeteria, a miniature golf course, a game arcade, a glassblower's shop, a T-shirt store, and a campground.

North of the chasm are some interesting wetlands, features one doesn't usually associate with the Adirondacks. The Ausable Marsh State Wildlife Management Area is popular with birdwatchers, especially during the fall migration. There is a state campground just beyond the wildlife-management area. As you drive along Lake Champlain, be on the lookout for the famed Loch Ness monster. Even Samuel Champlain claimed he saw an unusual creature during his original exploration of the lake in 1609. During the summer months, ferries run across the lake to Vermont.

HIGH PEAKS AND NORTHERN ADIRONDACKS

Lake Placid is the definite hub of the High Peaks and Northern Adirondacks area. American essayist William Burroughs called the High Peaks "the real Adirondack monarchs." Lake Placid Village has long described itself as the "Winter Sports Capital of the World" and has hosted two Winter Olympics—in 1932 and again in 1980. During the 1980 Olympics the Olympic Arena was the site of the much heralded "miracle on ice" when the American ice-hockey team beat the Soviet team to win the gold medal. Since the 1980 Olympics the resort village has become the home of the United States Olympic Training Center. Top athletes train and compete here year-round.

The Olympic Authority manages specialized facilities that include the Mount Van Hoevenberg Recreation Area, the Ski Jump Complex, the Speed Skating Oval, the Whiteface Mountain Ski Area, and the Whiteface Mountain Veterans Memorial Highway. The Authority offers a package plan featuring reduced-price admission to Mount Van Hoevenberg, the Olympic Ski Jump Complex, Whiteface Mountain Veterans Memorial Highway, and Whiteface Mountain Chairlift. The package is a bargain if you plan to visit all four attractions, but you will need more than a day to do so.

Whiteface Mountain in Wilmington is the highest skiing peak in the east and the only Adirondack high peak accessible by car. Ice has shaped the mountain, and the distinctive white slash on the mountain was created by avalanches.

Whiteface Mountain has its own Indian legend. The mountain's distinctive white markings are said to have resulted when an Indian brave slew the Great White Stag near its peak. Finding the terrain treacherous, the hunter returned to camp without his prize. The next day the stag had vanished, leaving his mortal whiteness behind as he disappeared to haunt the Adirondack forests.

A battle raged after World War I between environmentalists and the American Legion over the creation of a toll highway leading to Whiteface Mountain. The Legion felt that at least one peak should be available by car, and that the highway to it should be dedicated to New York's war dead.

In a 1927 statewide referendum, the voters agreed. In 1929 Franklin Roosevelt turned the first stone to start construction. He later returned to dedicate the Whiteface Mountain Veterans Memorial Highway.

The president, crippled by polio and standing with the aid of braces, looked out upon the vista and said, "Many persons, due to age or disability, cannot indulge in the luxury of camping or climbing. . . . For millions of people who have not got the facilities for walking up a mountain, we have now got the means for their coming up here on four wheels."

When the highway opened to the public on July 20, 1935, the first vehicle up the mountain was a seventy-five-year-old stagecoach that once carried mail and passengers between nearby Paul Smith's and Port Kent on Lake Champlain.

At a ceremony in 1985 celebrating the one hundredth anniversary of the forest preserve and the fiftieth anniversary of Whiteface Highway, a four-part plaque was unveiled honoring New York State veterans of all American wars. The plaque, now mounted near the summit, is the state's only memorial honoring veterans of all wars.

The highway climbs up an eight-mile stretch, terminating just 500 feet short of the summit. The road is open only in good weather, so a call ahead is advisable. There are lots of scenic pull-offs where you can pause to enjoy the views.

A stone castle near the main parking area at the top houses historic and scientific exhibits, a cafeteria, a gift shop, and many windows for viewing the surrounding countryside.

To reach the summit, most visitors take the elevator. Hardier individuals climb the Whiteface Mountain Nature Trail, three-fifths of a mile long. It sounds innocuous enough, but it's a hand-railed rocky footpath and a series of stone stairways along the outside of the final peak. Be sure to wear good walking shoes.

On a clear day, the view is unsurpassed. The panorama encompasses the Montreal skyline, Lake Champlain, Vermont's Green Mountains, and hundreds of Adirondack peaks and lakes. Renowned traveler Lowell Thomas described the view as "one of the great scenic vistas of the world."

The Whiteface Mountain Chairlift takes skiers and sight-seers high above the Olympic racing trails on a two-stage trip that involves switching lifts at the mid-station lodge. Eventually you will reach the peak of Little Whiteface. Be sure to allow about two hours for the round trip.

For a different kind of thrill, visit the Mount Van Hoevenberg Recreation Area, home of America's only bobsled and luge runs. The bobsled run is 1,600 meters long and drops 162 feet. The fastest run in the world, it has sixteen curves, including Shady Corner with a 170-degree change in direction. The deep concrete trough twists down the mountainside like a huge snake. Bobsleds, manned by two- or four-man teams, can reach speeds up to 90 mph in competitive events. Brave noncompetitors may ride on a bobsled Tuesday through Sunday from 2:00 to 4:00 P.M. during the winter season. You speed down from the half-mile start with a professional driver and brakeman on a ride considered the "Champagne of Thrills."

Mount Van Hoevenberg also has a luge run. The slider lies on his or her back on the narrow sled, head raised just enough to allow the slider to see. The sled has no mechanical steering or braking devices. The slider controls its passage through the ice trench with his or her feet and by shifting his or her weight. On weekend afternoons, rides are available on the luge through the final five turns.

If you visit in the off-season, you can walk around the bobsled and luge runs and take a truck ride up to the top of the mountain for a different perspective. If you visit in the winter, you can watch top athletes training and racing most days. In the finish-line buildings you can try out old sleds, luges, and other equipment and watch videos of earlier competitions.

There's a fifty-kilometer network of cross-country ski trails adjacent to the bobsled and luge runs. Skiing is almost always good from early December to late March.

Lake Placid is a year-round Olympic Training Center, and the year-round nature of the training is most apparent at the Olympic Ski Jump Complex, where plastic matting replaces snow on the jumps during the warmer months. Jumpers wear life vests, because after their jumps, twists, and somersaults they end up in a swimming pool, an unusual way to cool off on a warm summer day.

For a terrific view of the Adirondacks, step into the glass-enclosed elevator and head up the equivalent of twenty-six stories to the top of the ninety-meter tower.

Skating is available year-round at the Olympic Arena. Mirror Lake in the heart of the village offers tobogganing and dogsledding during the winter and is popular for canoeing in the warmer months.

Stop at Jones Outfitters Ltd. on the lake, where rowboats, canoes, and paddleboats may be rented by the hour, day, or week. If you are new to canoeing or inexperienced, you can join a guided day trip. Trips depart mornings and include lunch. The route involves a short portage over to Lake Placid; you'll have time for fishing and swimming before returning in the late afternoon.

Hiking is popular throughout the Lake Placid area. Trails are well marked, and access to the trailheads is easy. However, follow the rules of safe hiking. Do not hike alone, and be prepared for all weather conditions. The weather can change dramatically in the High Peaks.

The High Falls Gorge offers a different kind of hike. Privately owned and open from mid-May through mid-October, the gorge offers insight into the origins of the Adirondacks.

Nine locations are highlighted along the marked trail. Tapes explain the flora and fauna at each of the nine sites. More than 100 years ago, the vast majority of the trees of the Adirondacks were cut during mammoth logging operations. Most of the remaining trees were destroyed during two major forest fires in the

JOHN BROWN'S GRAVE

Many might be surprised to learn that the home and gravesite of abolitionist John Brown, immortalized in song ("John Brown's body lies a-mouldering in the grave"), are just outside Lake Placid Village.

Born in 1800, Brown had a strong belief that slavery was a sin against God. In 1849 he moved to this farm to assist in a plan formulated by abolitionist and philanthropist Gerrit Smith. The plan was to launch a self-sufficient community for free blacks. Smith owned more than 100,000 acres in the Adirondacks, and his plan was to give forty acres to each would-be homesteader.

Though the plan may have been born of noble ideals, it appears to have been doomed from the start. Not prepared for farming in the harsh climate, most of the residents left within a few years of their arrival. Brown himself lived on the farm only a few years. He abandoned his family for months at a time to pursue his antislavery concerns.

Brown is best known for leading an assault on the United States Arsenal at Harpers Ferry, West Virginia, in 1859. Trying to capture arms for use in the campaign to free Southern slaves, Brown was captured, convicted, and hanged for his participation in the raid. He and two sons who were killed in the raid on Harpers Ferry are buried on his farm, now a state historic site.

Brown's final prophecy: "I, John Brown, am quite certain that the crimes of this guilty land will never be purged away but with blood. I had, as I now think, vainly flattered myself that without very much bloodshed it might be done."

The neat cemetery on the Brown property is protected by a black iron fence. The house has been restored to its original appearance and is furnished in the style of a typical mid-nineteenth-century Adirondack farmhouse.

Ask the hostess for a free guide to the trail that begins at the pond just south of the farmhouse. A half-hour walk will take you through the fields and into the woods. The booklet identifies twelve species of trees commonly found in the Adirondacks.

Where: From Lake Placid Village, take State 73 south for two miles. The farm is located on John Brown Road, about three-quarters of a mile off State 73.

Hours: Wednesday through Sunday 10:00 A.M. to 5:00 P.M. mid-May through late October. Grounds open year-round.
Admission: Free.
Concessions: None.
Pets: Not allowed.
For more information: John Brown Farm, John Brown Road, Lake Placid, NY 12946; 518-523-3900.

---

early 1900s. A stand of forest in High Falls Gorge is one of the few remaining areas of virgin forest in the Adirondacks.

High Falls Gorge has a small restaurant, a gift shop, and picnic tables along the Ausable River, one of the famed trout streams of the Northeast.

Three miles south of Lake Placid Village is the Adirondack Loj, the Adirondack Mountain Club's wilderness retreat. You don't need to be a member of the club to stay at the Loj, but you must make advance reservations. Located on Heart Lake in the midst of the High Peaks, the 1920s-era lodge is a rustic, comfortable place with four private rooms, four bunk rooms, and a huge coed loft. Nearby, there's a wilderness campground for tents. Heart Lake has good swimming and fishing, and numerous hiking and cross-country ski trails are accessible from the property. Three backcountry cabins are accessible by foot—John Brooks Lodge, Grace Camp, and Camp Peggy O'Brien. Call 518-523-3441 for information and reservations. The Loj is open year-round.

ADIRONDACK PARK VISITOR INTERPRETIVE CENTER

Adirondack Park's two interpretive centers help visitors acquire a well-rounded understanding of the area. About half an hour north of Lake Placid on State 30, twelve miles north of Saranac

Lake, is the Adirondack Park Visitor Center at Paul Smith's. Through the center, everyone has easy access to the deepest secrets of Adirondack Park. This center focuses on the natural history of the Adirondacks.

The nearly 3,000-acre site adjacent to Paul Smith's College is leased from the college. The center offers exhibits and tourist information at a large building modeled after one of the park's legendary Great Camps. Interactive stations inform visitors about lodging, boat rentals, ski and hiking trails, even specifics such as the difficulty of a particular trail or the menu of a certain restaurant within the park.

Exhibits include a sensory trip through the Adirondacks' evolution in which visitors can feel the wind on the icy glacier that carved the mountains, see the mountains rise from the earth's crust, and end up at the edge of a trout stream. Audio-visual presentations are made in a 150-seat auditorium. A gift shop, a

**Loons are great divers whose diet includes fish as well as
mollusks, frogs, and aquatic insects**

lounge decorated with authentic Adirondack log furniture, and picnic areas complete the offerings at the main building. The new Butterfly House is a showcase for native species as well as the native plants on which they thrive. Visitors can see larvae, pupae, and adult butterflies in their native habitat.

The center's five and a half miles of trails are designed to allow visitors to complete one loop or all six at their own pace. The Easy Access Trail, which covers less than a mile, has a crushed-stone surface suitable for wheelchairs or strollers; a padding of shredded bark covers the others. If you take the Easy Access trail you will be treated to a close-up view of Heron Marsh and its population of great blue heron, beaver, and other birds and fish.

The Heron Marsh Trail offers an even closer look at the marsh. The trail leads to an observation tower and two board-walks at the water's edge. The half-mile Shinglemill Falls Trail takes walkers to the twenty-foot falls that give the trail its name. A bridge over the dam lets visitors stand above the falls for a spectacular view. Farther along, a 280-foot pontoon bridge crosses the marsh.

The mile-and-a-half Forest Ecology Trail focuses on the diversity of organisms in a forest community. This trail also fea-tures a boardwalk stretching 800 feet into the middle of a bog. The Boreal Life Trail covers just over a mile and demonstrates the qualities of a northern forest. The highlight is a 1,500-foot boardwalk through a tamarack and spruce swamp, landscape unique to northern regions.

South of Paul Smith's at Newcomb is the second Adiron-dack Park Interpretive Center. It's on State 28N, fourteen miles east of Long Lake and only half an hour from Blue Mountain Lake. The Newcomb center is adjacent to the Santanoni Preserve with its Great Camp complex on the shores of Newcomb Lake. Like the Paul Smith's center, it has an interpretive building with exhibits, park information, and special programs.

Winter visitors can borrow free snowshoes to explore the miles of trails. The Rich Lake Trail just beyond the interpretive building is surfaced for wheelchair travelers. The Peninsula Trail juts out into Rich Lake and features a boardwalk, as does the Sucker Brook Trail.

The 12,000-acre Santanoni Preserve, now deserted and empty, is owned by the state. Occasionally the Newcomb Center sponsors guided tours. This Great Camp was built from native logs in 1892 by a wealthy Albany industrialist, Robert C. Pruyn.

In the early days, Theodore Roosevelt was among the numerous guests who came to the camp to hunt and fish. The main camp complex includes a boathouse, a lakeside studio, and several buildings connected by some 5,000 square feet of veranda. You can peek in the windows of the main lodge and see the enormous fireplace and the birch-bark wallpaper.

More than 100 special events, workshops, and lectures are conducted annually at each center through the support of the Adirondack Park Institute. The institute also funds hands-on school programs, teacher-training workshops, curriculum development, a volunteer corps, internships, and the nationally syndicated radio program "Field Notes."

Both centers offer weekend classes in traditional Adirondack basket making, taxidermy, fly tying, watercolor painting, nature photography, and other skills. There are children's nature crafts programs on Saturdays.

Where: One center is at Paul Smith's on State 30, twelve miles north of Saranac Lake. The other is at Newcomb on State 28N, fourteen miles east of Long Lake and half an hour from Blue Mountain Lake.

Hours: Daily, year-round, except Thanksgiving and Christmas.

Admission: Free.

Best time to visit: July and August are most popular. The leaves

THE CLOUD SPLITTER

Mount Marcy, the highest and most celebrated of the forty-six Adirondack peaks over 4,000 feet, is sometimes known as Mount Tahawus, "the Cloud Splitter." Marcy is one source of the Hudson River at the poetically named Lake Tear-of-the-Clouds.

Marcy is popular with climbers. In fact, more than 10,000 climbers reach the peak each year. There's even a club for the more than 2,000 people who have climbed all forty-six High Peaks. Formed in 1937, the club developed into the Adirondack Forty-Sixers.

Before the Forty-Sixer name was coined, two New York City men, Robert and George Marshall, and their guide, Herbert Clark, had climbed all Adirondack peaks over 4,000 feet, completing their achievement together on Mount Emmons in 1925.

Octogenarian Grace Leach Hudowalski, the first woman to climb all forty-six peaks, has actually performed the feat at least twice since she began climbing the High Peaks at age fifteen. She is the keeper of the correspondence about the far-flung band of Forty-Sixers.

"The mountains change you," she says. "To me, there's a spiritual value in them."

---

are at their peak in late September. December, January, and February can be terrific for cross-country skiing with bright blue skies. March and April are generally mud season and least popular.

Activities: Tourist information, interactive displays, picnicking, hiking, nature walks, handicapped-access trails, weekend crafts classes, snowshoeing.

Pets: Not allowed in building. Allowed on trails on a leash.

For more information:

Interpretive Center at Paul Smith's, Box 3000, Paul Smith's, NY 12970; 518-327-3000.

Interpretive Center at Newcomb, P.O. Box 101, Newcomb, NY 12953; 518-582-2000.

NORTHWEST LAKES REGION

Paul Smith's on State 30 forms a border between the High Peaks area and the Northwest Lakes area. Tupper Lake is one of the best-known lakes of the Northwest Region. The town of Tupper Lake is a historic logging town where lumberjacks still compete each August in the Woodsman's Field Day.

Just north of Tupper Lake is Upper Saranac Lake, home of The Point, one of the most luxurious of the Great Camps. Don't expect to drop by for a look. The road is unmarked, and directions aren't given out unless you are a registered guest. If your bank account is large enough—a night costs more than $400, all meals included—you are in for the experience of a lifetime.

William Avery Rockefeller built this camp. It has been called simply the most attractive home in America that welcomes paying guests in the European tradition. The owners strive to give guests the sense of visiting a Great Camp during its heyday, pampering them with the most delicately prepared dishes and finest vintages. The Point is a member of the prestigious Relaix & Chateaux, the association of the world's finest restaurants and hotels. The atmosphere is of a truly elegant house party. *The Hideaway Report* called The Point "a private estate that sweeps all honors as the most enchanting lakefront sanctuary of its kind in America."

North of Upper Saranac Lake is Upper St. Regis Lake, at one time the social hub of the Adirondacks. It was here that Marjorie Merriweather Post entertained movie stars, heads of state, and friends and family at Camp Topridge. The living room has to be seen to be believed. The cavernous log hall is crammed with a no-longer-breathing menagerie of bear rugs; antler chandeliers; zebra-hide chairs; the jawbones of a whale; and heads of buffalo, bighorn sheep, moose, and deer waiting to charge off the wall. Inside Mrs. Post's private candy-striped bedroom cabin is her all-pink dressing room with heated towel racks and a pillow that reads, "Happiness is square dancing."

Paddlers agree that Adirondack Park offers some of the best canoeing and kayaking in the Northeast. The St. Regis Canoe Area is particularly prized by canoeists. It's possible to paddle for weeks on end and visit a different pond or lake each day. The canoe area, which includes much of Upper Saranac Lake, is off-limits to power boats. The fifty-eight lakes and ponds of this area are part of a vast network of interconnected waterways, linked primarily by the Raquette, St. Regis, and Saranac rivers. Check with St. Regis Canoe Outfitters (518-891-1838) for guided trips, canoe instruction, and car shuttles.

Cranberry Lake is the largest body of water in the relatively unexplored northwestern corner of the park. Several long and gentle hiking trails wind through the area around the lake.

The easy hike to a lookout from Bear Mountain provides a sweeping view of the lake and the countryside beyond. The trail up Bear Mountain starts at the 173-site Cranberry Lake Campground (315-848-2315). At Wanakena at the southern end of Cranberry Lake is the Ranger School.

CENTRAL AND SOUTHWESTERN ADIRONDACKS

The Central and Southwestern Adirondack region is one of the more popular and easily accessible areas of the park. Many of the park's important attractions are in this area – the Adirondack Museum, the Adirondack Park Visitor Interpretive Center at Newcomb, the Sagamore Institute, and the Fulton Chain of Lakes.

Blue Mountain – including lake, mountain, and village – is the geographical center of the Adirondacks. This tiny town with fewer than 200 year-round residents is one of those jewels that manage to remain true to themselves despite the thousands of visitors who pass through the town each season.

The cultural center of the region, Blue Mountain, is the home of the Adirondack Lakes Center for the Arts, which offers courses in a variety of crafts and presents plays, concerts, and films. At the crafts shop you can pick up handmade toys, baskets, pottery, prints, and other items made by regional artists and craftspeople. There are also lots of films and workshops for children. Intensive one- and two-day workshops are scheduled in photography, printmaking, weaving, calligraphy, woodworking, stained glass, basketry, batik, drawing, painting, pottery, and other crafts. Admission is free, although there are fees for performances and workshops. Phone: 518-352-7715.

South of North Creek is Gore Mountain, one of two ski mountains operated by the Olympic Regional Development Authority. (The other is Whiteface Mountain Ski Area.) Gore is the second largest ski area in the state, but it remains something of a secret among skiers in New York. Gore doesn't have as severe a climate as Whiteface, nor does it have the crowds of Hunter Mountain in the Catskills. Snowmaking covers much of the mountain, and there's a high-speed triple chair. With its wide-open cruising runs, trails have been widened. Gore is an ideal mountain for intermediate skiers. The mountain is home to New York's only gondola, which can be a real blessing on a blustery winter day.

The facility has an excellent nursery, a ski-and-play program for children three to six years old, and a ski school for all ages. Snowboarders are welcome, and there are even lessons for boarders. Call 518-251-2441 for information and snow conditions.

North Creek is also the whitewater hub of the Adirondacks and site of the annual Whitewater Derby in late May.

BLUE MOUNTAIN TRAIL

There are quite literally hundreds of hiking trails in the Adirondacks. One of the most popular and accessible trails is the route to the summit of the 3,759-foot Blue Mountain. It also gives hikers a feel for the other marked trails in the park.

The average hiking time for the four-mile round-trip on this trail is less than four hours. It would make a good half-day trip, even allowing time for a picnic on the summit.

A new trailhead north of the Adirondack Museum has replaced the traditional start, which crossed private lands. This new route saves about 200 feet of climbing. The trail follows a logging road for 300 yards to a sign-in booth. You will cross a stream on a half-log bridge, then begin a fairly steep climb through an especially beautiful wooded area.

Blue Mountain's trail is known for its steep pitches, which begin almost immediately. The route is worn to bedrock. The steep section levels out after about half an hour of climbing.

From the fire tower on the top, the views of lakes, ponds, and mountains are spectacular and hard to match in the park. Blue Mountain's isolation from surrounding hills makes for especially good viewing.

To the east you have my favorite view of Blue Mountain Lake and its sisters in the Eckford Chain. All three lakes were named by the surveyor Emmons for the daughters of Henry Eckford—Janet, Marion, and Catherine. Eckford first visited the lakes while participating in the 1811 state waterway survey.

The northeast face of the summit is bare, so it offers good views without a climb to the top of the tower. There is a picnic table north of the tower.

More than 100 years ago, the summit of Blue Mountain was the center of surveying efforts to produce an accurate map of the Adirondacks. Observations were synchronized each night at nine, when a charge of gunpowder was set off to alert observers on distant summits and coordinate their efforts.

The return trip follows the same trail. Be careful, because parts are quite steep and rugged.

Spring is the time when the real whitewater daredevils like to take to the river, because the water is highest after the runoff from the snow melt. The most popular runs are along the Indian River from Indian Lake and then to the Hudson River leading to North Creek. Hudson River Rafting Company (Main Street, North Creek, 518-251-3275) is a leading whitewater outfitter.

The drive between Long Lake and North Creek on State 28N is one of the prettiest in the Adirondacks, with mountain and lake views along the way.

To the west is the famous Fulton Chain of Lakes. This is also prime canoe country. The haunting call of a loon, a shy deer peeking from the alders along the shore, a sly mink scooting along a river bank, a picnic on a beach that is all your own, and the sight of some of the most colorful hardwood stands in the state are all part of a day spent canoeing a slow-moving river or wilderness lake in Adirondack canoe country.

For a true wilderness experience in only half a day, take a leisurely paddle down the North Branch of the Moose River. This is a four-hour trip for most canoeists, and it provides a real Adirondack experience.

The trip begins at the North Street Bridge near Old Forge. If you look at an aerial photograph of this section of the North Branch, it looks like a long, tangled skein of rope made out of multiple channels and byways. But the river is easy to follow, despite the dozens of narrow twists and turns, because underwater grass bends with the current and points the way.

As you paddle down the North Branch, you will pass dozens of tiny sand beaches ideal for a picnic. And you will pass through wetlands where the grasses hide numerous birds. In the fall, great stands of hardwoods splash their crimson, copper, and gold leaves against a palette of blue sky, evergreen-draped hills, and dark, towering hemlocks.

On this trip there is one portage where you have to stop,

take your canoe out of the water, and carry it around rapids or a waterfall. This 300-yard carry is on a well-marked trail that crosses a wooden bridge—where you get a good view of the massive boulders and narrow, foaming channels of Indian Rapids—and continues through some woods to a place where you can safely put in again and continue your downstream trip into the town of Old Forge.

Nick's Lake, a small lake with pristine beaches and forested shores just two miles from Old Forge, is perfect for novice paddlers and a good alternative for those who doubt their ability to negotiate the spaghetti-like North Branch of the Moose.

Old Forge is the center of tourist activity in the southern Adirondacks, but its amusements are low-key in comparison with those of Lake George.

Campsites are plentiful throughout this part of the Adirondacks. Best of all, most sites are on lakes—beautiful lakes such as Fourth Lake, Raquette Lake, Eighth Lake, Indian Lake, and Sacandaga Lake. Reservations can be made for a site in the state campgrounds by calling 1-800-456-CAMP. Campsites generally cost between $8.00 and $14.00 per night.

If you would like to try camping but don't know where to begin or don't own a single bit of equipment, the Beginner Camper Program sponsored by recreational equipment companies and the State Department of Environmental Conservation (call 914-255-5453 or 518-897-1309) is an easy way to learn the ropes.

If you wish to take to the water but don't own a boat and want someone else to serve as captain, there are a number of options in this area. Blue Mountain Lake Boat Livery (518-352-7351) offers cruises through the Eckford Chain of Lakes aboard two restored wooden launches accommodating eighteen or fewer passengers. Old Forge Lake Cruises (315-376-6200) offers a narrated twenty-eight-mile cruise on the Fulton Chain of Lakes aboard the *Uncas* or the *Clearwater*. Raquette Lake Navigation Company (315-354-5532) has lunch, brunch, and dinner cruises aboard the new *W. W. Durant*, an enclosed replica of a nineteenth-century boat.

Just about every lake has at least one marina with boats for rent and freely dispensed information about good routes and where the fish were biting yesterday.

Guides have a long tradition in the Adirondacks. Ralph Waldo Emerson praised the guides as "doctors of the wilderness" in his poem "Red Flannel." William H. H. Murray, who introduced tourism to the region, declared his usual guide, John Cheney, a paragon of virtue and described the independent guides themselves with great enthusiasm: "A more honest, cheerful, and patient class of men cannot be found the world over. Born and bred, as many were, in this wilderness, skilled in all the lore of woodcraft, handy with the rod, superb at the paddle, modest in demeanor and speech, honest to a proverb, they deserve and receive the admiration of all who make their acquaintance."

The Adirondack Guides' Association was established in 1891 as a kind of trade union. Now the Department of Environmental Conservation licenses hundreds of men and women for all kinds of outdoor recreation. Guides must pass a written exam and have current first-aid and CPR certification. Some 300 guides are members of a select group within the DEC licensees, the New York State Outdoor Guides Association. These guides are dedicated to helping clients find the right places for hunting, fishing, camping, and climbing. Many guides also practice low-impact camping and offer outdoor education.

For a list of the association guides and their specialties, contact Brian McDonnell, All Seasons Outfitters, PO Box 916A, Saranac Lake, NY 12983, 518-891-1176. For people with limited time, a guide can be a worthwhile investment. We have had fishing guides for half a day or a whole day who knew where the fish were biting and what they were biting. A guide is particularly good if you want to introduce children to the sport. After a day or so with a guide, you will probably feel more confident to go off on your own.

5

Thousand Islands and Lake Ontario

MARY ISLAND STATE PARK

The Thousand Islands are noted for privately owned islands with massive summer camps on them. But in Mary Island State Park in the middle of the Thousand Islands, our spot on the river seemed as close to perfect as it could be. By a stroke of luck we had the island to ourselves in the morning, although other campers and boaters arrived later in the day.

This is angler's heaven, and our pre-breakfast fishing foray had been successful. Now the walleye were frying up for breakfast, a day on the St. Lawrence River stretched before us, and the weather gods were with us. We felt that even the owners of the beautiful private estates across the water didn't have better prospects.

The St. Lawrence River is extremely popular for fishing. Many species are present, including largemouth bass, northern pike, walleye, smallmouth bass, muskellunge, and many others.

It is often difficult for newcomers to know if they are in Canadian or American waters here, but be aware that a New York or Ontario fishing license is required—depending on where you are fishing. Penalties are stiff if you are caught without a license.

Mary Island is a real jewel in the Thousand Islands region. What makes living or camping on an island special is the sense of escape it imparts. The road here is the river, just as it was hundreds of years ago. The supermarket is not just down the road. Since the island can be reached only by boat, crowds are rare. The island has thirteen acres—all state land. The fourteen camping sites on the perimeter of the island are all forested, well spaced, private, and close to the water, so there is a real feeling of getting away from it all here even when the park is full.

Muskies feed where weeds border deep waters

The season for camping is late May through Labor Day. The picnic area is open all year, but there are no rest rooms open after Labor Day. There are ten picnic tables with cooking stations near the main dock, if you are visiting just for the day. The three docks are shared by campers, picnickers, and people staying overnight on their own boats. Some campers tie up their boats in front of their campsites. A sewage pumpout station is provided.

A narrow channel separates Mary Island and Wellesley Island. The main dock and day-use area for Mary Island is near the channel. This pleasant, grassy area overlooks the river, which is two and a half miles wide at this point. A protected cove to the north is popular for picnicking and relaxing.

Where: Mary Island is on the St. Lawrence River, northwest of Alexandria Bay. People usually launch from Keewaydin State Park, about two miles away. The main dock facility at Mary Island is on the southwest corner of the island.

Hours: The picnic area is open all year, but the rest rooms are open only from late May through Labor Day.

Admission: $9.00 per campsite and $3.00 for day visitors.

Best time to visit: Summer.

Activities: Camping, picnicking, fishing.

Pets: Must be on a leash.

Other: There are no shelters, play areas, recreation programs, or lifeguarded swimming areas.

For more information:

Mary Island State Park, RD 2, Box 166, Clayton, NY 13624; 315-654-2522.

Campsite reservations, 800-456-CAMP.

WELLESLEY ISLAND STATE PARK

The 2,636-acre Wellesley Island State Park near Alexandria Bay in the Thousand Islands is an ideal family park, offering something for just about everyone—except those seeking solitude.

The parklands were originally an operating farm owned by Edison Bradley of New York and Washington. Bradley was the owner of the Old Grand Dad Distillery and the Bradley Horse Stables. After buying the farm in 1906, he named it "Arcadia." With his farm manager, George Houghton, he set about making the farm as self-sufficient as possible. Ayrshire cattle and Shropshire sheep were raised on the farm, as well as chickens and pigs. Bradley put in place a major reforesting project, planting hundreds of trees. Berry fields and grape arbors were planted in nearby fields. Evidence of Bradley's efforts can still be seen today.

During the summer of 1911, construction was begun on a seasonal home high on the cliff over the present bathing beach. This home was one of the first built on the northern part of the river and accessing the Canadian Channel. At the time, newspaper articles referred to the structure as a "bungalow." Though descriptions varied, it is commonly believed that the "bungalow" measured 240 feet by 68 feet, containing forty rooms, nine baths, and wraparound porches. An eighty-foot water tower was attached to the second floor by suspension bridge, and electricity for lighting was provided by Bradley's own Delco power plant.

As was the case with many estates in the Thousand Islands, Bradley's bungalow was destroyed by fire in 1922. Sparks from the chimney set the roof ablaze and in just two hours the entire house was gone. After the fire, Bradley built small structures on an island off the point, but the family didn't visit the area often. Eventually he sold the property to Paul Houghton, who furnished the island with milk and other dairy products and started the area's first "rescue service," towing cars that became mired in the mud on the one-lane roads of the island.

In the early 1950s, the Thousand Islands State Park Commission purchased the farm and other parcels to develop Wellesley Island State Park, which was opened to the public in 1954 with 100 campsites and ten cabins. The park has grown considerably over the years, now offering 429 campsites, ten winterized cabins, a nature center, hiking trails, a nine-hole golf course, a marina, a picnic area, a beach camp store, and a recreation barn. There's a natural sand beach with a lifeguard during the summer.

A highlight of the park is the Minna Anthony Common Nature Center, which includes a museum and wildlife sanctuary. The center is named in honor of the late Minna Anthony Common, a leading authority on the birds, flowers, trees, animals, herbs, and grasses of northern New York State. Her nature writings and pen-and-ink illustrations were published for twenty-five years in the Watertown *Daily Times* prior to her death in 1950. Mrs. Common was a summer resident of the Thousand Islands all her life. She developed and maintained Rock Ledges Nature Trail next to her property. The one-and-a-half-mile walk through the woods was popular with visitors and school groups who were able to identify various natural elements through trail markings placed by Mrs. Common. The Thousand Islands State Park Commission voted unanimously to name the nature center in her honor as a tribute to her pioneering work in promoting nature education.

The center encompasses a 600-acre peninsula on the southeast end of Wellesley Island State Park. The terrain varies from steep cliffs and exposed rocky knobs to more gentle landscapes with wetlands, meadows, and forests. It is bordered by Eel Bay, The Narrows, and South Bay on the St. Lawrence River, a location that provides spectacular views.

The nature center is housed in a high-ceilinged modern building. It is dedicated to conserving natural resources, promoting environmental awareness, and providing recreational programs. The museum features displays of the St. Lawrence River's environment, geology, and native flora and fauna, along with a touch table. Living collections include native fish, reptiles, amphibians, and an observation hive of honeybees. Facilities for the public and for scheduled groups include a reference library, an audio-visual room, and two well-equipped classrooms.

Interpretive naturalists conduct a variety of activities daily from the last week of June through Labor Day. These activities include an Ecology Canoe Paddle, guided hikes, children's activities, family campfire programs and games, camp skills, guest speakers and camping-skills slide presentations, workshops, and a concert series.

A special feature of the center is the quarter-mile Friendship Trail developed through the efforts of the Clayton Lions Club and the Thousands Islands State Park Region. Designed for wheelchair use and the visually impaired, it is marked with interpretive signs in raised letters. Located along the trail are a rest station, a listening post, an herb garden, and a geology wall containing interesting rocks and minerals to touch.

There are five other well-marked trails here — ranging from a half mile to 3.5 miles. We chose the two-and-a-half-mile Eel Bay Loop with scenic views of Eel Bay. The trail follows the bay to The Narrows along forested sandstone ledges and open crystalline rocky knobs. Climb the hill above The Narrows for two overlooks of the river and descend the other side of the knob down the steps to the Mid-Narrows Trail. Turn inland and take the Mid-Narrows Trail to the Middle Trail and return to the museum.

Although the nature center and park attract the biggest crowds during the summer, activities continue throughout the year. On one visit in October, we were greeted by a field full of scarecrows dressed in an array of costumes. They had been created as part of the annual autumn festival.

During the winter, seven miles of cross-country ski trails are maintained. Ski-equipment rentals and free snowshoes are available for use on site. The museum's fireplace helps warm outdoor explorers. Bring along a picnic and purchase cocoa, soup, and coffee on the spot.

Where: The entrance to Wellesley Island State Park is reached by following State 12 to the Thousand Islands International Bridge, between Alexandria Bay and Clayton.

Hours: The park and nature center are open year-round. The nature center is open weekends from November 1 through April 30 and weekdays by appointment during that time. It is open daily the rest of the year.

Admission: $4.00 per car from late June to Labor Day, free otherwise.

Best time to visit: During the summer, activities operate daily and the park is at its most crowded. September and early October can be beautiful in the Thousand Islands, and the fishing is usually excellent then. The marina is open May through October.

Concessions: The park has a store and a marina. Boats are available for rent. Bait and tackle are available, too—everything you need to land yourself a bass, a northern pike, or even a muskie. There's a nine-hole golf course for which tee times may be reserved two days prior to intended play. There's also a mini-golf course and a ninety-slip dockage.

Activities: During the summer, concerts, folksingers, story-tellers, and other performers, plus a recreation center. During the winter, there's ice fishing, cross-country skiing, and snow-shoeing. There are special events throughout the year: Art Show in August, Autumn Festival in October, Trim-the-Tree Party in December, Winter Festival in February, and Earth Day Spring Festival in April.

Pets: Household pets are allowed in a cage or on a leash. Proof of a current rabies certificate is required.

For more information:

Wellesley Island State Park, 44927 Cross Island Road, Fineview, NY 13640; 315-482-2722.

Nature Center, 315-482-2479.

Golf course, 315-482-2722.

Campsite reservations, 800-456-CAMP.

SELKIRK SHORES STATE PARK

Though there's no aroma of salt air, it's easy to mistake Lake Ontario for the ocean. Standing on the beach at Selkirk Shores State Park, you see just miles and miles of water and the horizon—no comforting shoreline. Lake Ontario, one of the Great Lakes, borders the park on one side. On two other sides of the park are the Salmon River and Grindstone Creek. Water is clearly predominant here.

During the fall, the Salmon River is one of the hottest spots in the country for salmon fishing. You can expect large crowds of fishing enthusiasts there. There is a fish-cleaning station at the park. Be sure to follow the Health Department advisories regarding consuming the fish.

A passage connects the Salmon River and Lake Ontario. However, there is no overnight docking or mooring at Selkirk Shores. Boaters generally dock at private marinas or pull their boats out at night. Canoeists use the Salmon River and Grindstone Creek for short trips. Storms can come up quickly on Lake Ontario, and rough water is not uncommon on the lake, so boaters with small craft should be careful.

There are 150 campsites here, each with a picnic table and a fireplace. Most of the campsites are in open or lightly forested areas, although ten are set amidst trees that afford some privacy. There are also twenty-four cabins.

During the summer, a staffed recreation program is provided, including a sandy beach, a bathhouse, and a lifeguard. The park has about six miles of flat trails through woods and open areas. Wildlife is abundant, and deer can often be seen at dusk near the trails. During the winter, cross-country skiing and snowshoeing are popular, and parts of the park roads are plowed for access.

The park has a recreation building, a camp store, boat

rental, and a children's area, as well as a large picnic area with more than 400 tables and eighty cooking stations in a forested area near the beach. Several of the campsites, bath areas, and cabins are handicapped-accessible.

Where: Take State 3, four miles southwest of Pulaski, which is just off I-81.

Hours: Camping and other services are provided from late April through mid-October. The park is open the rest of the year for skiing or other activities, but no facilities are open from late October through April.

Admission: $4.00 per car for day use during the summer season; camping is $10.00 per night.

Best time to visit: During the summer if you want to take advantage of swimming and the beach. September and early October can be beautiful if the weather cooperates.

Activities: Camping, picnicking, boating, canoeing, fishing, cross-country skiing, snowshoeing, nature trails, children's area.

Pets: Allowed on a leash with proof of rabies vaccination.

For more information:

Selkirk Shores State Park, RD Route 3, Pulaski, NY 13142; 315-298-4010.

Campsite reservations, 1-800-456-CAMP.

6

Western New York

NIAGARA FALLS

It is, as always, an awesome spectacle: a sprawling 182-foot-high cataract of thundering water, surrounded by towering clouds of mist and spray.

There may be taller cataracts in Africa, South America, and even elsewhere in New York State, but the sheer size and tremendous volume of Niagara are unsurpassed. Contrary to popular opinion, Niagara Falls is not listed as one of the Seven Wonders of the World. Still these falls are a wonder. It is the combination of height and volume that makes them so beautiful and wondrous.

For generations, Niagara Falls has been the stuff of romance. If the vaunted honeymoon connection has become a cliché these days, the lure that made it so has not. More than 11,000,000 visitors pause here each year to witness one of the world's most impressive natural phenomena. They line the promenade opposite, gape from the deck of a boat below, peer out from the caves behind, ogle from a helicopter above — drinking in the vista from every conceivable angle.

It's hard to believe it wasn't always thus, but in 1985 the world celebrated a century of unrestricted viewing of Niagara Falls. Before 1885, the lands around the falls had become one of the most vulgar tourist traps anywhere, with visitors having to pay for the privilege of seeing the cataract.

It was undoubtedly the peepholes that offended the most. The land belonged to private owners who charged visitors a fee to view the mighty cataract through holes in their fences. Americans—many of whom had never visited the falls but had seen them in Frederic Church's well-known painting—found it upsetting that visitors had to look through peepholes to view such magnificence.

By the mid-1800s, Niagara Falls had become a victim of one of the ugliest assaults on a wonder of nature with the growth of factories, shacks, and mills around the cataract. The insult of having to pay to view the falls helped generate a most ingenious lobbying and public-relations campaign. It had one goal: Free Niagara.

Spurred by this rallying cry, the Free Niagara Movement—a group of Americans including landscape architect Frederick Law Olmsted—returned the area around the falls to its natural state and to the people of the world.

The campaign resulted in the establishment, on July 15, 1885, of the nation's first state park, embracing 435 acres of land along American Falls. The Canadians followed with similar action around their portion of the cataract, and the falls' protection was assured. However, the fight against overcommercialization continues to this day.

To create the nation's first state park, serious legal obstacles had to be overcome. Never before had a state attempted to appropriate private land for purely aesthetic purposes.

The first people known to suggest that Niagara Falls be preserved were two Scottish clergymen who visited in 1834. The

Reverends Andrew Reed and Thomas Mattheson wrote: "Niagara does not belong to Canada or America. Such spots should be deemed the property of civilized mankind: and nothing should be allowed to weaken their efficacy on the tastes, the morals and the enjoyment of all mankind."

It was a Canadian, Lord Dufferin, governor general of Canada, who gave the Free Niagara campaign the boost it needed in an address in 1878, when he criticized "the various squatting interests that have taken possession of every point of vantage at the Falls; who tax the pockets and irritate the nerves of the visitor."

Lord Dufferin went on to urge preservation of the falls in "the picturesque and unvulgarized condition in which they were originally laid out by the hand of Nature."

The first tourist to witness the wonder of the mighty Niagara Falls was Father Louis Hennepin, who served as a missionary under French explorer Robert LaSalle. After seeing the falls on a cold December day in 1678, Father Hennepin wrote an eyewitness account and revealed to the world for the first time the "incredible Cataract or Waterfall, which has no equal."

In a book widely read across Europe, Hennepin wrote: "Betwixt the Lake Ontario and Erie, there is a vast and prodigious Cadence of Water . . . the Universe does not afford its Parallel. . . . The Waters which fall from this horrible Precipice do foam and boyl after the most hideous manner imaginable, making an outrageous Noise, more terrible than that of Thunder."

Nearly two centuries later, novelist Charles Dickens wrote: "I seemed to be lifted from the earth and to be looking into Heaven. Niagara was at once stamped upon my heart, an image of beauty, to remain there changeless and indelible."

Mark Twain simply wrote: "Niagara Falls is one of the finest structures in the known world."

Thomas Moore, the Irish poet, declared: "It is impossible by pen or pencil to convey even a faint idea of their magnificence. . . . We must have new combinations of language to describe the falls of Niagara."

"Niagara Falls! By what mysterious power is it that millions and millions are drawn from all parts of the world to gaze upon Niagara Falls? . . . It calls up the infinite past," said President Abraham Lincoln.

However, not every writer was overwhelmed by the falls. Oscar Wilde was singularly unimpressed on his visit. In 1883 he said he was "disappointed with Niagara—most people must be disappointed with Niagara. Every American bride is taken there, and the sight of the stupendous waterfall must be one of the earliest, if not the keenest disappointments in American married life."

Wilde's comments notwithstanding, there is a mystical, magnetic, alluring, and even hypnotic quality to the hundreds of thousands of gallons of water pouring over the brink every second.

All these rave reviews began to bring out the professional daredevils as well as the amateurs. In 1859 the great French tightrope walker Blondin walked across Niagara Gorge, from the American to the Canadian side, on a three-inch-thick rope. On his shoulders he carried his reluctant, terrified manager; on both shores stood some 100,000 spectators. "Thank God it is over!" exclaimed the future King Edward VII of England, after the completion of the walk. "Please never attempt it again."

A seasoned circus performer, Blondin displayed his showmanship when he decided to sit down on the rope and have a drink halfway across the gorge. He kept up his performances all summer, thrilling onlookers as he walked, danced, rode a bike, and carried his manager across.

Others tempted the falls. From the early eighteenth century, daredevils went over in boats, rubber balls, and those famous barrels. Schoolteacher Annie Taylor survived her plunge over the falls in 1901. Emerging from her barrel, she asked, "Did I go over the Falls yet?" Although the stunts were finally outlawed, people continue to challenge the falls to this day.

The falls are part of the longest unfortified border in the world and are actually three cataracts: American and Bridal Veil Falls on the American side, and the nearly half-mile-wide Horseshoe Falls on the Canadian side. American Falls is half the width of Canadian Falls, but still quite impressive. The international boundary between Canada and the United States is in the middle of the Niagara River, below the falls.

Goat Island—part of the state park—offers the closest possible views of American Falls and the upper rapids. To the Native Americans who lived here hundreds of years ago, Goat Island was regarded as sacred because it touched both American and Horseshoe Falls. It was considered the ultimate place of honor for burial.

Altogether, Niagara Falls has 3,175 feet of waterfall. The falls were the birthplace of alternating electric current, and they drive one of the largest hydroelectric developments in the world.

The water that flows over Niagara Falls drains four Great Lakes—Superior, Michigan, Huron, and Erie—into the fifth, Ontario, at a rate of 700,000 gallons a second during the summer. The waterfall fluctuates with the season; although the river never completely freezes in winter, an ice bridge often forms below the falls—a bridge that can grow to 150 feet thick and two miles long.

On March 29, 1848, a strange silence fell in the city of Niagara Falls. The roar of the falls had stopped. Huge chunks of ice had formed a dam in the river, stopping the flow of water and leaving the falls dry. This situation lasted for two days, until the dam broke and water began to flow again.

On June 12, 1969, the falls—actually just American Falls—were turned off again, this time by humans. Water was rerouted to Horseshoe Falls so that engineers could survey American

Falls and the rocks below to study ways to prevent further erosion. Some 185,000 tons of rock had fallen from Prospect Point over the years. In December, the falls were turned back on, and they have been flowing steadily since.

Any of the many vantage points here can confirm Mark Twain's view of the falls, but perhaps the most vivid experience involves the *Maid of the Mist* boat ride. It has been in operation more or less continually since 1846.

President Theodore Roosevelt called the ride "the only way fully to realize the Grandeur of the Great Falls of Niagara." It has become as much a symbol of Niagara as the falls themselves. There are now four *Maid of the Mist* boats, which can be boarded every fifteen minutes on either side of the falls for the thirty-minute ride.

It is hard to imagine a more intense experience of the power of the falls than this ride into their base. The captain expertly guides the boat past the base of American and Bridal Veil Falls and almost into the thunderous deluge of Horseshoe Falls.

The roar of the cataract drowns out the drone of the vessel's two 250-horsepower engines. Spray stings the face and hands and blurs vision. The boat rocks as the engines fight for control in the current. The captain knows he must stay in the middle, because the back eddy close to the Canadian shore could suck the boat into the falls. There is a moment on the trip, just a moment, when the world seems to be coming to a watery end.

Of course, it is all perfectly safe, and only once has one of the *Maids'* cork life preservers been used. Back in the summer of 1960, seven-year-old Roger Woodward was swept over the falls after a boat he was in stalled and broke up on the rocks near the brink. He plunged 161 feet over the falls at a speed of some seventy-five miles an hour. He was wearing an orange life jacket, so passengers spotted the child quickly and threw him the preserver. Plucked from the turbulent waters, he became the

MAID OF THE MIST

The *Maid of the Mist* cruise is one of the oldest tourist attractions in the United States and Canada. It takes its name from an Indian legend perpetuated by the Senecas, who inhabited the Niagara frontier in the 1600s.

First told to French priests who came to the area in 1678, the legend has ever since been a mystical part of Niagara Falls.

Here's how it goes: Long ago, the peaceful tribe of the Ongiaras lived beside the Niagara River. For an unknown reason, Indians were dying. It was believed that the tribe must appease the thunder god, Hinum, who lived with his two sons in a cave behind the falls. At first, the Indians sent canoes laden with fruit, flowers, and game over the falls, but the dying continued. The Indians then began to sacrifice the most beautiful maiden of the tribe, selected once a year during a ceremonial feast. It was an honor to be selected. One year, Lelawala, daughter of Chief Eagle Eye, was chosen.

On the appointed day, Lelawala appeared on the riverbank above the falls wearing a white doeskin robe and a wreath of woodland flowers in her hair. She stepped into a white birchbark canoe and plunged over the falls to her death. Her father, heartbroken, leaped into his canoe and followed her. Hinum's two sons caught Lelawala in their arms, and each desired her. She promised to accept the one who told her what evil was killing her people. The younger brother told her of a giant water snake that lay at the bottom of the river. Once a year, the monster snake grew hungry and entered the village at night to poison the water. The snake then devoured the dead.

In spirit, Lelawala told her people to destroy the serpent. Indian braves mortally wounded the snake on his next yearly visit to the village. Returning to its lair in the river, the snake caught its head on one side of the river and its tail on the other, forming a semicircle and the brink of Horseshoe Falls.

Lelawala returned to the cave of the god Hinum, where she reigns as the Maid of the Mist.

only person in history to survive a plunge over the falls without a protective device. Woodward returned to the falls twenty years later on his honeymoon to view the cataract from a more conventional angle.

Where: Niagara Falls, New York: base of observation tower at Prospect Point and across the river in Niagara Falls, Ontario; Maid of the Mist Plaza, elevator at foot of Clifton Hill. Take New York Thruway to Niagara Falls exit. From Canada, take Niagara Parkway and the Rainbow Bridge to falls.
Hours: 9:00 A.M. to 8:00 P.M. in summer, otherwise 9:00 A.M. to just before dusk.
Admission: $7.00 for adults, $3.50 for children six to twelve, free for children five and under, plus fifty cents for state observation-tower fee, which is necessary to reach landing. Fee includes use of hooded rain coats.
Best time to visit: Anytime. I love a hot summer day when I can enjoy the cooling spray.
Pets: Not allowed.
For more information:
   Maid of the Mist, 151 Buffalo Avenue, Niagara Falls, NY 14303, 716-284-8897; or dock during the season, 716-284-4233.

The Cave of the Winds offers another perspective on the falls. Visitors buy tickets and don yellow slickers and felt slippers. After a short elevator ride, a guide takes the group through a tunnel in the rock—not the Cave of the Winds proper, which has been closed for years since a series of rock falls, but a very reasonable substitute.

A web of wooden catwalks and staircases takes visitors to numerous points where the view is quite astounding. Rainbows abound here. The last stop, Hurricane Deck, is just twenty-five feet from Bridal Veil Falls. Prepare to get wet—the spray and mist are ever-present.

Tour guides offer tales of the past. A Pennsylvania couple was married here in 1893, almost within touching distance of Bridal Veil Falls. More recently, a Korean tourist was smacked in the face by a fifteen-pound Chinook salmon trying to leap up the waterfall. It was undoubtedly a dead heat over the question of who was more surprised.

On the Canadian side, Journey Behind the Falls (formerly Table Rock Scenic Tunnels) offers close-up views of Horseshoe Falls. Wearing yellow slickers, visitors go down 125 feet by elevator into dank tunnels. There are 650 feet of underground caverns here. Take one of the tunnels to a two-level observation deck at the side of the falls for a fish-eye view and feel of the cataract. Two other tunnels lead to viewing portals behind the "mighty curtain of water." Here you will feel the power and presence of Niagara.

It's customary to throw a coin into the water from here, and on the Duke of York's visit in 1987 his guide jokingly invited him to throw his mother into the water. (The queen's face is on all Canadian coins.)

There are other ways to see the falls—helicopter flights, cable-car rides, towers with fine vantage points, even a revolving restaurant that serves up unmatched views. There's hardly a means of observation that hasn't been devised and offered here—for a price. Olmsted's vision of natural beauty untarnished by man has yet to be achieved, although today is a vast improvement over the pre-1885 days.

In Whirlpool Rapids, several miles below the falls, you can see the "reversal phenomenon." When the Niagara River is at full flow, the waters travel over the rapids and enter the pool, but then travel counterclockwise around the pool, past the natural outlet. Pressure builds up when the water tries to cut across itself to reach the outlet, and this pressure forces the water under the incoming stream. The swirling waters create a vortex, or whirlpool. Then the waters continue their journey to Lake Ontario.

If the water level is low because of diversion for hydroelectric purposes, the reversal does not take place; the waters merely move clockwise through the pool and pass to the outlet.

The attractions have their serious side. The Schoellkopf Geological Museum, within view of American Falls, has a multiscreen audio-visual theater presentation that explains the 500-million-year story of Niagara Falls. Perched on the edge of Niagara Gorge, the museum offers panoramic views from several overlooks. A geological garden at the rear of the museum displays fossils, minerals, and rock structures extracted from the gorge.

For an up-close view of the gorge, take a free guided tour offered by the museum. Walks vary from pleasant meanders along the rim to more difficult and steep descents—to the edge of the rushing Niagara River, to the level of the great whirlpool, or to the base of the falls themselves to feel the vibration of their thundering power and be showered with spray.

The tours are designed to be educational and fun. If your time is limited, Niagara Reservation State Park takes visitors to Prospect Point, Goat Island, Luna Island, Terrapin Point, and the Three Sisters Islands. In two and a half hours, your guide will describe the formation of the falls, identify plants along the paths, and describe the creation and development of the nation's first state park. Walks and nature programs generally depart from the museum. They are free, but pre-registration is required.

Where: Schoellkopf Geological Museum, on state parkland a few hundred yards north of American Falls.
Hours: 9:00 A.M. to 5:00 P.M. daily. Closed Monday through Wednesday during the winter months.
Admission: Free.
Best time to visit: Anytime.
Activities: Guided nature walks and tours throughout the year, nature talks.

Pets: Not allowed.

For more information:
Schoellkopf Geological Museum, Niagara Reservation State Park, PO Box 1132, Niagara Falls, NY 14303; 716-278-1780.

A centerpiece of downtown Niagara Falls is a shimmering 107-foot-high glass and steel steeple-shaped tropical green-house – the Wintergarden. Visitors can stroll under forty-foot palm trees and wander through 225 different varieties of plants, all labeled with their botanical and common names. It is a popu-lar spot for weddings, and during a busy Saturday in spring or summer there are often four or five weddings here.

Although many attractions (such as the *Maid of the Mist* and Cave of the Winds tours) generally operate from May through October, Niagara Falls is still very much a year-round natural wonder. There is an enchanted quality to Niagara Falls on a winter night, when thousands of lights glisten off the spray-iced trees. The falls are illuminated every night, adding to the sense of wonder and beauty.

Since 1981, Niagara Falls has sponsored a Festival of Lights beginning Thanksgiving weekend and continuing into January. There are large displays of lights on both sides of the border, fireworks, parades, entertainment, buggy rides, and a multitude of animated displays. Outdoor displays on the sides of buildings on the American side include the nine-story-tall Oxy-Lights, recognized by the *Guinness Book of World Records* as the world's largest light-sound synthesizer, and the Nabisco Fantasy of Lights display of moving lights and music on the 180-foot-tall silos of Nabisco Brands.

If your past visits to the falls have been during warm weather, a winter visit during the festival presents the falls in an entirely new light – actually tens of thousands of them.

For an inside view of the falls that doesn't require a raincoat, take in "Niagara Miracles, Myths and Magic" in the Niagara Falls Imax Theater adjacent to the Skylon Tower on the Canadian side. On a screen ten times the size of a normal theater screen, the film takes viewers back to the days when Native Americans worshipped the thunder beings, 2,000 years before the first Europeans discovered the falls. You'll also meet the daredevils who challenged the fury of the falls, including The Great Blondin and Annie Taylor.

At the visitors center in Niagara Reservation State Park, there are daily screenings of *Niagara Wonders*, which captures the falls from every possible vantage point and provides a brief look at the area before the modern-day tourist invasion.

The visitors center is the place to go for information, exhibitions, the T-shirt or ashtray of your dreams, and a café with indoor and outdoor seating overlooking Prospect Point.

Flower lovers should head across the Rainbow Bridge to Canada to view the 100 acres of beautifully manicured flower gardens designed and maintained in the English tradition by the students at the famed Niagara Falls School of Horticulture. The Niagara Parks Greenhouse, just a quarter-mile south of the falls, is open daily year-round. All the 135,000 bedding plants that are used for the many colorful gardens planted each year in the falls parks are grown in this greenhouse.

Outside, there's a delightful fragrance garden. The plants are labeled in braille for the convenience of the blind.

Be aware: if you get sidetracked on Clifton Hill just off the falls on the Canadian side, you will find yourself in one of the tackiest and most garish areas of souvenir stands and museums in all of North America.

Between mid-April and mid-May the city of Niagara Falls, New York, promotes the Golden Festival, centering on the more than 1,000,000 daffodils that have been planted in the past few years.

For a different view of the falls, drive six miles north to the

New York State Power Authority Visitors Center. The Power Authority produces some of the lowest-cost electricity in the world and today accounts for about fourteen percent of New York State's total electrical supply. When the Power Authority built the plant in 1958, the mission was to develop the river's energy fully and to maintain the 1950 U.S.–Canadian treaty designed to preserve the beauty of the falls. They diverted water out of the river two and a half miles above the falls, then channeled it through four miles of underground tunnels to the plant several miles below. The placement of the project at a strategic point maximizes the river's momentum, enabling it to spin thirteen gigantic waterwheels or turbines.

At the visitors center there's a breathtaking view of the gorge—350 feet straight down. Exhibits in the center imaginatively show just how hydroelectricity works. On the upper level, exhibits explain other energy resources, including hydro, nuclear, solar, fossil fuels, and technologies of the future. One of the area's finest art treasures is here also—a mural depicting Father Louis Hennepin's visit to the falls. American artist Thomas Hart Benton painted this masterpiece to celebrate the completion of the Niagara Power Project.

ARTPARK

Niagara Falls originated some 12,000 years ago and seven miles north of its present location, in what is now the village of Lewiston. Lewiston is now best known for Artpark, which opened in 1974. The only state park in the nation devoted to the visual and performing arts, Artpark encompasses 200 acres along the Niagara River.

A historic site, this is where Seneca Indians, French, British, and Americans fought for control of the strategically important Niagara River. After the American Revolution, Lewiston thrived as a center of trade and transportation. The town was burned by the British in the War of 1812 and rebuilt within two years. Here also are relics of Hopewell Indians who lived on the site 2,000 years ago. A burial mound thirty feet long, twenty feet wide, and five feet high is listed in the National Register of Historic Places.

At Artpark, you can sit at the feet of a storyteller in the woods, don a mask and join a company of actors, watch your child create a puppet, or try your hand at oriental brush painting. Nightly concerts and plays are staged by the Buffalo Philharmonic Orchestra, touring companies, and big-name entertainers. The grass seats are inexpensive, and you can bring a picnic or order one ahead of time and pick it up at the park. It's hard to beat listening to beautiful music while enjoying a picnic and watching a magnificent sunset over the river.

There are well-marked paths down to the river and easy access for fishing enthusiasts. Salmon are frequently caught here.

Unfortunately, because of advisories regarding chemical contaminants in the river, you are urged to check with the Health Department or the Department of Environmental Conservation before consuming the fish taken here. Many enjoy the challenge of fishing, landing the catch, and promptly releasing the fish to challenge another angler.

Where: Lewiston is seven miles north of Niagara Falls. Take the Robert Moses Parkway to the Lewiston exit. Follow signs on State 104.

Hours: 9:00 A.M. to evening; open until after performances on performance nights.

Admission: $3.00 parking fee. There are charges for some daytime arts activities; otherwise admission is free. Concert and performance charges range from $6.50 for lawn seating to $37.50.

Best time to visit: Summer to experience the full range of Artpark programs, throughout the year for hiking and fishing.

Activities: Artists-in-residence, visiting-artists program, performing-artists program, workshops and studio classes, college courses, Elderhostel, children's camp programs, including a program for children 6–12 who can attend for a day or afternoon at a time. There are twice-daily Culinary Workshops with area chefs at the park's Log Cabin Kitchen.

Concessions: Picnics ordered in advance, snack bars, refreshment stands, a gift shop.

Pets: Not allowed.

For more information:

   Artpark, 150 South Fourth Street, Box 371, Lewiston, NY 14092; 716-754-9000.

FORT NIAGARA STATE PARK
AND OLD FORT NIAGARA

The thirty-five-mile-long Niagara River empties into Lake Ontario at Youngstown, site of Fort Niagara State Park and home of Old Fort Niagara. The fort is within the state park but operated independently of the park. The flags of three countries — France, Britain, and the United States — have flown over this fort. The fort's original stone building, French Castle, is the oldest building in the Great Lakes area. Fort Niagara controlled access to the Great Lakes and had early commercial importance in the beaver trade. There is a self-guided tour of the fort grounds. Military reenactments, battles, grand reviews, tent camps, fife and drum concerts, crafts, and archaeological digs are scheduled throughout the year.

   The area of the park that includes the fort and the Fort Niagara Lighthouse is one of the longest continuously occupied military sites in North America. The French explorer LaSalle built Fort Conti in 1678, and the last army units left in 1963. After the Revolutionary War, Americans posted a garrison in 1796.

   The park has picnic areas, tennis courts, and soccer fields.

Winter sports include snowshoeing, cross-country skiing, and snowmobiling. There is a sledding hill for sleds and toboggans. Two boat launches provide access to the Niagara River. Anglers may try their luck in the river or in Lake Ontario for game fish and panfish, including coho and Chinook salmon; brown, lake, and rainbow trout; and white and smallmouth bass. Other additional species here are northern pike, walleye, yellow and white perch, bullhead, catfish, smelt, and carp. Waterfowl hunting is allowed in the park with a permit.

Though there isn't any overnight camping at Fort Niagara, you can camp at Four Mile Creek Campsite from mid-April to mid-October.

Groups of painted turtles bask on favorite logs and slip into the water at the slightest hint of danger

The campsite, just four miles east of Fort Niagara along the Lake Ontario shoreline, offers 266 camping sites spread throughout the 248-acre campsite. There's no evidence to be found today in the calm and serene marsh of Four Mile Creek, but back in 1759 this marsh played a critical role during the French and Indian War. The British, with 2,200 soldiers and 900 Iroquois warriors, put to shore at the mouth of the creek to lay siege to Fort Niagara. After eighteen days, the French surrendered the fort—a turning point in the war.

The marsh area provides a habitat for many types of wildlife. You may be able to see great blue herons, chipmunks, eastern painted turtles, or muskrats. The largest trees are oaks, some of them more than 200 years old. Wildflowers abound, including white trillium, trumpet honeysuckle, greenbrier, and many more.

Where: Fort Niagara is 17 miles north of Niagara Falls on State 18F. Take Robert Moses Parkway to Youngstown.

Hours: Old Fort Niagara is open daily 9:00 A.M. to 4:30 P.M. Summer hours are 9:00 A.M. to 7:30 P.M. The park is open daily.

Admission: The park charge of $3.00 applies only in the summer. Old Fort Niagara charges $6.00 for adults and $3.75 for children 6–12, year-round.

Best time to visit: During the summer you can see the Old Fort Niagara Guard fire muskets and cannons in drills. There's an ongoing archaeological dig at the fort that visitors can see during the warmer months.

Activities: Boat launches, fishing, tennis, swimming, soccer fields, cross-country skiing, snowshoeing, snowmobiling.

Concessions: Gift shop at fort.

Pets: Allowed on a leash in park; not allowed at fort.

For more information: Old Fort Niagara, Fort Niagara State Park, Youngstown, NY 14174; 716-745-7611 (fort), 716-745-7273 (park).

FOUR MILE CREEK STATE PARK

Where: Four miles east of Youngstown.
Hours: Daily, mid-April to mid-October.
Admission: Campsites are $12.00 to $14.00 per night.
Best time to visit: Summer is most popular, but if the weather gods are with you late September and early October can be particularly beautiful and are less crowded.
Activities: Hiking, play areas, fishing.
Pets: Allowed on leash or in cages.
Other: Laundry facilities and hot showers are available.
For more information: Four Mile Creek State Campsite, Box 275, Route 18, Youngstown, NY 14174; 716-745-3802.
Campsite reservations, 1-800-456-CAMP.

PANAMA ROCKS

Panama Rocks is a place of mystery and fascination for me. This private park, filled with massive rocks and caves, always seems to remain cool and green. I first visited on expeditions from a nearby summer camp—a favorite jaunt.

Children, particularly, love the natural labyrinth of caves and deep crevices here. Some caves are dark and spooky, but daylight is always near. There are cool breezes from the caverns and moss-hung nooks.

There is history to these rocks. The Eries and later the Iroquois sheltered among them, storing their meat in ice caves deep in the ridge. The Native Americans believed in the power of stones or rocks of the "rock cities" such as Panama. Gwylah Nitsch, president of the Seneca Nation Historical Society, recalls that it was her grandfather, Moses Shongo, last of the Seneca medicine men, who told her of the ancient power in stones. The Stone People are the oldest living things, she believes.

Even if you don't believe in the power of the stones, these megaliths have a presence.

Local legend has it that a gold shipment is buried somewhere here, supposedly hidden and then lost by the robbers of a Clymer, New York, bank.

According to the park brochure: "It is said that outlaws used the rocks to hide their ill-gotten loot. Once a courier carrying a gold shipment to the Clymer bank was waylaid. The gold was supposed to have been dropped into a deep hole in the rocks at night. When the robbers returned, they could not find the gold because there were so many holes. An organized search ensued, but was suddenly abandoned. The man in charge of the search was suspected of being one of the robbers. To this day it is written up as being one of the ten best treasures in the East."

If you find any gold nuggets, you must turn them in at the gates upon leaving.

Panama Rocks originated as sand-and-gravel beaches and bars, along the shore of an ancient inland ocean. They were part of the delta of a great river, larger than the Mississippi. The formation began more than 300 million years ago, during a time known as the Age of Fishes, when animal life was beginning to emerge from the seas and the first forests were starting to spread over the land masses. The primary life forms at that time were marine mollusks and corals; fossils of these forms of sealife have been found here.

Contrary to popular opinion, the rocks were not deposited by the glacier. In fact, rock cities characteristically occur in the only part of New York State not transformed by the glacier. This triangular-shaped region in the Southern Tier, which includes Allegany State Park, is known geologically as the Salamanca reentrant.

By the turn of the century, the rocks had acquired a reputation as a lovers' escape because of the many concealed niches in the rock, away from prying eyes. The attraction was also a popular honeymoon retreat. Panama Rocks has been operated as scenic park since 1885.

The Panama Rocks Folk Fair runs for three days, starting the second Friday of July. The fair features more than 100 exhibits and demonstrations, including basketry, blacksmithing, broommaking, cannon firing, decoy carving, dollmaking, dulcimer and other old instrument design, furniture making, painting and drawing, pottery creation, quilting, sewing, spinning, sheep shearing, stained-glass work, woodworking, weaving, and more.

There are frontiersmen, mountain men, and eighteenth-century militia encampments, along with a variety of frontier crafts and artifacts. Live bluegrass music is performed daily.

In October the Panama Rocks Foliagefest is held to celebrate autumn, when the spectacular scenery of the rocks is at its colorful best. This two-day event is staged the first or second weekend in October. There is live bluegrass music each day. Some of the exhibits from the folk fair return. There are horse-drawn wagon rides through the forest. Food is available.

Panama Rocks has a one-mile trail. Visitors can explore off-trail and discover passageways, caverns, and caves. Wear sneakers or other comfortable footwear. Bring flashlights for exploring the caves and dens. Photographers should bring a wide-angle lens and fast film. Children must be closely supervised. There are no railings, and many tree roots cross the trail. Strollers cannot be pushed along the trail.

Where: Panama Rocks is located one-quarter mile west of the light in Panama. Take State 474 west; turn south onto Rock Hill Road. Panama is five miles south of exit 7 off State 17, the Southern Tier Expressway. It is ten miles south of Chautauqua Institute, fourteen miles west of Jamestown, and thirty-five miles east of Erie.

Hours: 10:00 A.M. to 5:00 P.M. daily, May to mid-October.

Admission: $5.00 per adult, $3.00 for children 6–12, $4.00 for senior citizens.

Best time to visit: May and June for wildflowers, fragrances, and a great variety of birds; summer to enjoy the coolness of the rocks and caves; late September and early October for the play of red, yellow, and brown leaves against the massive rocks.
Activities: Cave exploration, picnicking, wildflowers, bird-watching, folk fair, nature trail.
Concessions: Picnic area and snack bar. Alcohol and radios are limited to the picnic area.
Pets: No dogs or other pets are permitted anywhere on the grounds.
For more information:
   Panama Rocks, Panama, NY 14767-0176; 716-782-2845.

ALLEGANY STATE PARK

"Here where pioneer conditions and the native Indians survive, the people may come for rest and recreation."

   This inscription over the massive stone fireplace in the Tudor-style administration building proclaims the mission of Allegany State Park, New York's largest park outside the Adirondacks and Catskills.
   An inscription on the opposite wall recalls an earlier era: "These historic and abandoned forests, once so important and productive, shall again and for all time survive the uses and betterment of mankind."
   In 1873 Amasa Stone Jr. purchased 7,000 acres of land in the southwestern area of New York for $40,000 from John S. Casement, intending to build a private game preserve. The game preserve was never realized. After a number of owners and administrators, the Stone estate was purchased in 1904 for oil speculation by the Land & Petroleum Company. The impetus for a state park on these lands was due, in large part, to the efforts of Senator Albert T. Fancher of Salamanca. The park came into

The burnished green head, red eye patch, and white neck ring of the male pheasant outshine the quiet plumage of the female

being on May 2, 1921, after the governor appointed a five-member commission, headed by Sen. Fancher, to develop a vast park of 65,000 acres to be called "the wilderness playground of Western New York." The park actually opened with 7,150 acres of land on July 31, 1921. Land acquisition continues even today, so the park now comprises more than 65,000 acres on the Pennsylvania border.

Camping in the summer of 1921 was quite different from what visitors see today. The first park headquarters was a converted schoolhouse, and the first campers used World War I surplus tents pitched on wooden platforms. It was 1925 before the first permanent cabins replaced the tents.

The Civilian Conservation Corps, which operated from 1933 to 1942, was responsible for much of the early development of the park. CCC workers built roads, bridges, and picnic and camping areas, and completed numerous conservation projects, including forestation, stream-bank retention, and wildlife improvements.

Today the park operates under a policy that tries to balance recreational development with the control and protection of wildlife and other natural resources. It is a beautiful and wild land with mountains, streams, and lakes. The Erie and Seneca Indian Nations once lived here; *Allegany* is an Indian word meaning "beautiful waters."

This region is rich in oil, the production of which contributes more than $55,000,000 to the state's economy each year. Oil and gas wells are located in the park and throughout the area. The first oil well in the state was drilled in 1865 near the village of Limestone at the southeastern edge of the park.

Despite Allegany's popularity, it's possible to find solitude here. It's also possible to see deer, wild turkeys, pheasants, raccoons, and even bears. Other animal residents are opossum, beavers, muskrats, rabbits, weasels, porcupines, skunks, foxes, and squirrels—even timber rattlesnakes.

Don't worry about the snakes; shy creatures that like rock crevices, they are rarely sighted. Be careful around all wild animals, as rabies has been found throughout this part of the state.

Although the busiest season here is summer, the park is very much a year-round attraction, with a variety of activities throughout the year. It is glorious in the fall, when the hills are ablaze with color. During the hunting season, deer, turkey, and other game may be hunted in selected areas with proper permits. Fishing is allowed year-round, including ice fishing in the winter. A special, free permit is required.

Red House and Quaker are the two main recreational areas. A newer, smaller area, Cain Hollow, opened in 1971. Red House has 144 cabins, of which eighty are winterized for year-round occupancy. There are also campsites for tents and trailers. The cabins are small green cottages, each with a front porch. They are primitive, with no indoor plumbing, but they do have refrigerators, cooking ranges, and wood stoves, as well as cots and mattresses.

Allegany State Park has nearly seventy miles of hiking trails. The shortest jaunt is Bear Springs Trail, a leisurely half-mile walk off Park Route 1. Most park trails range from two and a half to five miles.

Stop at the Red House administration building for a trail map. Constructed in 1927, the building houses the rental office, a restaurant, administrative offices, a camp store, and a small natural-history museum. This is the place to ask questions and get directions.

Three of the park's hiking trails, the Finger Lakes Trail, Hiking Trail #4, and the Red Jacket Nature Trail, begin behind the building on the hill. The small weather station behind the administration building includes a barometer, a wind gauge, a maximum-minimum thermometer, and a gauge to measure precipitation. Just a short hike from the administration building is Bridal Falls. Though not a spectacular waterfall, it is beautiful in spring and fall, when rainfall increases the trickle to a cascade.

Although you might spot animals at any time, dusk is the best time for cruising the park roads in search of wildlife. Deer are more active at this time than earlier in the day, and beavers begin their night of activity as the sun goes down. Bats begin to fly at dusk. If you can put aside the normal fears many people have of bats, you will find it fascinating to watch their aerial antics as they feed on flying insects. During one half-hour drive through the park in the early evening, we spotted three deer, a woodchuck feeding along the road, and several raccoons.

As you drive or walk in the park, look for holes along the road. Eaten out by deer, these holes are always associated with saltwater seepage. Deer are attracted to them for the salt.

Horses are welcome in the park. On our last visit we encountered a group of trail riders who came complete with their own pack llama. The old logging roads make good trails for the horses.

Beyond Bridal Falls, a scenic overlook provides a good view of the park. This region, along with much of eastern North America, was covered by ocean waters 350 million years ago. Sediments deposited on this ocean bottom subsequently were hardened into rock and uplifted to form a plateau. Notice the even skyline formed by these mountaintops at about 2,400 feet above sea level. Water erosion has carved the plateau through succeeding ages and formed the V-shaped valleys typical in the park.

The park is unique in having escaped the bulldozing effects of the Wisconsin Glacier. During the Ice Age that began 2,000,000 years ago, four major glacial advances and retreats occurred. In the last advance, the mile-high Wisconsin Glacier covered all of New York except the land that now makes up Allegany State Park. The park is the most northerly region of eastern North America that was not covered by the glacier.

This vantage point also provides a good overview of Allegany's woodlands. The north- to northwest-facing slopes are covered with the typical northeastern hardwood forest of sugar maple, beech, red maple, yellow and black birch, and hemlock. The forest on the south-facing slopes represent the Appalachian hardwood group. Oaks and hickories are the main species, with cucumber, tuliptree, white ash, and black cherry here as well. Seedlings of the Appalachian hardwood group need sunny openings to develop. Because of the thick overstory in most of the Allegany woodlands, the hardwoods are being replaced by beech, maple, and hemlock seedlings, which are tolerant of shade.

Guided tours of the park's bear caves are available; we made the trek on our own. It's a short uphill hike from the Quaker Run area. The large blocks of rock here are Salamanca conglomerate, characterized by flat white quartz pebbles in a more finely grained matrix. Salamanca conglomerate is believed to be a beach deposit, with pebbles flattened by washing back and forth in the surf. It is debatable whether bears use the caves here. Bears are seen in this area from time to time, but we didn't spot any during our trek.

The park's Nature Interpretive Program operates year-round through a variety of hikes led by trained naturalists who interpret the natural world of the park. We chose a "Tour of a Beaver Colony." Our guide led us to the beaver pond, where we saw how the beavers had dammed the small stream. The pond is surrounded by clumps of small willows and alder shrubs. Aspen are normally found around beaver colonies, but this pond's dam builders have cut all the nearby aspens. Beavers are strict vegetarians who eat a lot of bark as well as water lilies, cattail roots, and various other aquatic plants.

We saw the beaver lodge made of sticks cemented by mud. The beavers hollow out the dome and live above the waterline on a shelf that circles the inside.

Our guide told us that beavers at the park normally bear two kits per year, and a typical colony has a family group of six. Two of these are the parent beavers, two are yearlings, and two are young kits. In areas where the food supply is plentiful, as many as five kits may be born to a pair of beavers each year. When the young beavers are two years old they leave to establish colonies of their own and select mates.

In the winter, beavers do not hibernate but are active under the ice. They store a supply of small branches near the lodge to use as their winter food supply.

Recreation opportunities abound in the park throughout the year. During the summer, activities include swimming in the lakes, sunbathing on the sand beaches, fishing, and boating. You may rent fishing poles and purchase bait at the park. Rowboats and paddle boats may be rented at the boathouse next to the miniature golf course in the Red House area. Only electric boat motors are permitted on Quaker Lake. There are tennis courts here, and volleyball, and softball facilities, as well as biking trails and rental bikes. The park offers organized campfire sing-alongs as well as outdoor movies and down-home hootenannies. Naturalists provide guided hikes and programs throughout the year. During the summer, more than ten activities are scheduled daily, including fossil hunts, a bird walk, a star watch, and even a twenty-five-mile bike trip. Hunting and fishing are allowed with park permits.

During the winter there are more than fifty-five miles of snowmobile trails that weave back and forth across the park and connect with the Allegheny National Forest in Pennsylvania. Another thirty miles of trails in the Summit area make up the Art Roscoe Cross-Country Ski Trail system, perhaps the best in the entire state. The ski area includes a warming hut, and rental equipment is available. The park staff grooms the trails on old logging roads and on the track bed of an 1890s narrow-gauge railroad.

Cross-country ski competitions and a Winter Fun Fest for snowmobilers are augmented by dog-sled competitions throughout the winter months.

Where: Allegany State Park is on the southern boundary of New York, west of Olean and east of Jamestown. You can enter the park from State 17, exit 18 or 19, or from US 219 in Salamanca. A less-traveled entrance is in Limestone in the southeast corner of the park.

Hours: Year-round, twenty-four hours a day. The administration building is open daily, 9:00 A.M. to 5:00 P.M.

Admission: For day use, $3.00 admission per car from Memorial Day weekend to Labor Day weekend; during the swimming season, $4.00 per car. From the fourth Saturday in June until the last Sunday in August, all cabin rentals must be made for a full seven nights; at other times, there is a two-night minimum rental on cabins.

Best time to visit: Anytime, depending on your interests. Summer is the most popular, but winter is increasingly popular. Fall is especially lovely and popular with hunters.

Activities: Hiking, hunting, snowmobiling, skiing, fishing, swimming, boating, bicycling, camping, natural-history museum, horseback riding, guided nature trails.

Concessions: Three restaurants, bicycles, rowboats, and paddleboats for rent. A boat-launch area offers access to the Allegheny Reservoir. There are snack bars at the beaches and a camp store in the administration building.

Pets: Dogs and cats are permitted in camping area, but they must be constantly restrained by a leash not exceeding six feet, or kept in a cage. Owners must present proof of current rabies inoculation.

For more information:

Allegany State Park, RD #1, Salamanca, NY 14779; 716-354-9121.

Camping reservations, 800-456-CAMP. Reservations are not taken more than 90 days in advance. However, make them as soon as possible, since the cabins and campsites are very popular.

Allegany State Park is surrounded on three sides by the Allegheny Indian Reservation. Salamanca, just outside the park entrance, has the distinction of being the only city in the country entirely on Native American lands. The land is owned by the Seneca Nation.

The park also borders the Allegheny Reservoir and River—part of the reservation lands. The Seneca Nation operates Highbanks Campground, offering camping and RV accommodations overlooking the reservoir.

The campground provides an alternative to camping in Allegany Park. It offers fishing, a boat launch, a swimming pool, private tent and RV sites, and fifty cabins.

Where: Highbanks Campground, Steamburg. Take State 17 to exit 17, then go south on State 394 for three miles.

Hours: Open year-round. Day visitors must be out of the campground by 10:30 P.M.

Admission: $3.00 per person for the day, otherwise rental charges range from $10.00 per night for nonelectric sites to $40.00 per night for cabins.

Best time to visit: Summer and early fall.

Activities: Swimming, fishing, boating, a nine-hole mini golf course, playground, picnicking, recreation center.

Concessions: General store and laundry facility. Seneca Nation fishing licenses are available here and are required by all non-Indians. Three-day permits are $5.50. Senior citizens and disabled persons pay only fifty cents.

Pets: Allowed if kept on a leash.

For more information:

Highbanks Campground, PO Box C, Steamburg, NY 14783; 716-354-4855.

ROGER TORY PETERSON
INSTITUTE OF NATURAL HISTORY

More than sixty years ago, in 1934, Roger Tory Peterson published his first *Field Guide to the Birds*. This is the book that introduced the Peterson identification system and has become the "birder's bible." It has sold more than 5,000,000 copies.

Born in Jamestown, New York, Dr. Peterson has spent the past seventy years in pursuit of the beauty of nature — particularly birds. In 1993, when Peterson was 85, the new headquarters of the institute named in his honor was dedicated in his hometown. He is a trustee and honorary chairman of the institute. The mission of the Roger Tory Peterson Institute of Natural History is "to inform society about the natural world through the study and teaching of natural history."

The institute's goal is to create passion and concern for the natural world in the hearts and minds of children, the future stewards of the earth. "We must reach all mentors of children— their teachers and those who teach the teachers," said Dr. Peterson. "We must give them the tools and instill in them a responsibility, in their young charges a knowledge and love of nature."

Workshops and training sessions for teachers are held regularly in Jamestown and at many locations across the United States, as well as in Mexico. The nature-education programs developed and implemented by the institute's staff focus on classroom teachers, parents, youth leaders, and others who have the desire to teach children about the natural world.

Special forums are scheduled each year. Forums have focused on nature education for young children, urban nature education, the needs of nature centers, nature photography, and the contributions of wildlife art to understanding and appreciation of the natural world. The institute hosts nature photography workshops for classroom teachers, students, and children. There are special tours and activities for children.

An art gallery and a library with space for 40,000 volumes are two important components of the new building. One of the institute's goals is the creation of an outstanding collection of literature in the field of nature and environmental education for children and young adults. Nature art and nature photography have been two important components of Dr. Peterson's educational work.

The design of the 23,000-square-foot institute in itself demonstrates a relationship between the building and the natural environment. It symbolizes the work of Dr. Peterson and all wildlife artists and their concerns about the natural world.

The fieldstone exterior and rough-sawn siding on the building, as well as the use of wood interiors, complement the meadows and woods that surround it. The setting—a twenty-seven-acre wooded site on the edge of the city of Jamestown in Chautauqua County—is appropriate. Jamestown is a community of 34,000 people nestled among the rolling hills in the southwestern corner of New York. The region retains the rural character that Dr. Peterson knew as a boy, with woods and fields to roam in search of birds, butterflies, and moths. Here Roger Tory Peterson began the journey that led to his love for the birds he has painted, photographed, and written about for seven decades.

The most celebrated naturalist of our time, Peterson has received every award in the field of conservation, including the Audubon Conservation Medal from the National Audubon Society. In 1980 he received the Presidential Medal of Freedom.

Dr. Peterson has summed up his philosophy and the focus of the institute: "The philosophy that I have worked under for most of my life is that the serious study of natural history is an activity which has far-reaching effects in every aspect of a person's life. It ultimately makes people protective of their environment in a very committed way. It is my opinion that the study of natural history should be the primary avenue for creating environmentalists."

Where: 311 Curtis Street, Jamestown, off State 60 South. Follow the signs to Jamestown Community College.
Hours: Tuesday through Saturday 9:00 A.M. to 5:00 P.M.; Sundays 1:00 P.M. to 5:00 P.M. during special exhibits. Closed Mondays.
Admission: $3.00 adults, $2.00 senior citizens, $1.00 children and students.
Best time to visit: Anytime, but especially during special exhibits.

Activities: Nature education, nature photography workshops, library, art gallery, children's activities.

Concessions: The gift shop offers a wide selection of *Peterson Guides*, posters, photos, and other nature-related materials.

Pets: Not allowed.

For more information:

Roger Tory Peterson Institute of Natural History, 311 Curtis Street, Jamestown, NY 14701; 716-665-3794.

TIFFT NATURE PRESERVE

From the deck of the log cabin that extends close to the edge of the lake, you see Canadian geese and mallard ducks swimming by. In the distance, there is a great blue heron. Nearby, several young boys fish for bass or anything that bites. Experiencing this scene, it's very easy to fool yourself into thinking that you are in the wilds of the Adirondacks. But this is Buffalo's Tifft Nature Preserve, just off the Skyway and in the shadow of grain elevators and former steel mills.

This 264-acre nature preserve, a unique urban sanctuary, is a tribute to the concerned citizens who fought for its creation. It certainly could serve as a model to other cities of a successful instance of recycled wasteland. Wild plants and animals are abundant here. Birds, especially, are attracted to the wetlands, near Lake Erie's coastline.

The land that makes up Tifft Nature Preserve has an interesting history. Once part of a huge dairy farm owned by George Washington Tifft, it later became a transshipment center, first for livestock and then for coal and ore. During the 1950s and 1960s, Tifft Farm was a dump for city refuse.

The transformation of Tifft to a nature preserve began in the 1970s. Nearly 2,000,000 cubic feet of solid waste was enclosed in clay and covered with soil excavated from another section of the preserve. Ponds were enlarged and trees and wild-flowers planted. Conservation of Tifft's large cattail marsh helped attract a variety of animals. The preserve opened in 1976 and in 1982 became a department of the Buffalo Museum of Science.

The parking lot is next to Lake Kirsty, which is home to a large flock of Canada geese. Smallmouth bass, perch, trout, and bullheads swim in this lake and other lakes and canals. The peculiar shape of the lake is the legacy of the Lehigh Valley Rail-road, which dredged these canals out of the Tifft Farm wetlands in the 1880s to create a transshipment terminal. Thickets and early-stage forests on the peninsula across the lake have replaced trestles and railroad sidings. Ducks and other waterfowl now float on Lake Kirsty in place of lake freighters.

Close by is the Makowski Visitor Center, built in the style of a log cabin. It is named in honor of the late Stanley Makowski, a Buffalo mayor who pushed for the creation of the preserve. The center offers exhibits on ecology, animals, and plant life along with a "touch me" table and lists of recent sightings of birds and animals. Red fox, cottontails, muskrats, and raccoons are among the preserve's permanent residents. Field guides are available here, and classes are held in the center.

The seventy-five-acre cattail marsh is the preserve's most significant natural feature, a remnant of the extensive wetlands that once bordered the eastern end of Lake Erie. A marsh is a wetland characterized by soft-stemmed plants such as cattails, water lilies, and coontail; swamps, on the other hand, are charac-terized by woody plants such as trees and shrubs.

The domes of cattails and mud protruding from the marsh are made by muskrats. The animals do most of their construction in late summer, since these houses are their preferred wintering sites. They also use bank dens. Like beavers, muskrats enter and leave their houses below the water surface. Their primary food is plant matter, especially cattails, but they will also eat animal

**Canada geese can be found in lakes, bays, rivers, and marshes,
sometimes feeding in open grasslands or stubble fields**

matter, such as fresh-water mussels. In the North, muskrats typi-
cally produce two litters of young per year, with about seven
young per litter.

Look across the marsh for a sight that captures the essence
of Tifft Preserve. Although the land has a history of use and
abuse by man, now nature and man have found a peaceful co-
existence here. The large factories you see are now silent.
They were formerly occupied by Republic Steel and Donner-
Hanna Coke Company. The Cargill "S" elevator, one of the
Buffalo River's historic grain elevators, shadows the north end
of the marsh.

A former railroad bed has been transformed into a trail called Rabbit Run in honor of the eastern cottontails often seen feeding here in the early morning and late evening.

On a recent visit, I continued along Rabbit Run to the North Viewing Blind. Ahead of me were a swimming muskrat and several herons on Lisa Pond. Others have seen pied-billed grebes, American widgeon, blue-winged teal, moorhens, coots, and other ducks and waterfowl. The area of open water has been created by muskrats removing the cattails.

Nearby is Beth Pond, part of the eastern canal of the Lehigh Valley transshipment terminal. An iron-ore dock was formerly located between the eastern canal and this railroad bed. The red soil along this trail, often showing reflective metallic chips, is the residue of iron ore moved between the ore dock and railcars decades ago.

Continuing back toward the visitors center, you can walk along the Nettle Trail, aptly named. The trees that rise from the nettles are trees of heaven. Native to northern China, the tree of heaven was introduced to the United States from England in 1874. It is the hardiest of urban ornamentals, able to withstand smoggy air and the nutrient-poor and dry soils along city streets. The tree inspired *A Tree Grows in Brooklyn*, by Betty Smith.

Where: Three miles from downtown Buffalo, 1200 Fuhrmann Boulevard. Take the Skyway or Ohio Street to Fuhrmann Boulevard and get off at the Tifft Street exit. Follow signs.
Hours: Daily, sunrise to sunset. The Makowski Visitor Center is open Tuesday through Sunday, 9:00 A.M. to 5:00 P.M. Closed January 1, Thanksgiving, December 24 and 25.
Admission: None.
Best time to visit: Anytime.
Activities: Snowshoeing, cross-country skiing, classes and field trips, fishing, picnicking, sleighrides and hayrides. During the winter snowshoes are available for rent and you can bring your

own cross-country skis. There are free guided nature walks every Sunday at 2:00 P.M., and during the winter the walks are conducted using snowshoes. There are sleigh- and hayrides in season. Classes and field trips are held regularly in the preserve. They include a marsh exploration, Twilight at Tifft, a beaver hunt, frogs and pollywogs, birding for adults and children, wildlife identification, Tifft After Five, and animal-track identification. Fishing is popular, although successful anglers should read the posted notices about eating their catch, since this was once a garbage dump. Most people catch and release the fish. There are picnic tables near the visitors center but no facilities for camping or cooking.

Concessions: Snowshoes can be rented. Field guides, books, and maps are available in the visitors center.

Pets: Not allowed.

For more information:

Tifft Nature Preserve, 1200 Fuhrmann Boulevard, Buffalo, NY 14203; 716-825-6397 or 716-896-5200.

IROQUOIS NATIONAL WILDLIFE REFUGE

It's early April at the Iroquois National Wildlife Refuge, and the marshes and swamps are alive with thousands of geese. Overhead are thousands more birds. This is not a quiet place. In fact, it can be downright noisy with the musical calls of the waterfowl across the fields and marshes.

The refuge is part of Oak Orchard Swamp, a pristine tract of some 19,000 acres of wetland just forty miles northeast of Buffalo. The 10,818-acre Iroquois Refuge shares Oak Orchard Swamp with its neighbors, the Tonawanda State Wildlife Management Area to the west and the Oak Orchard State Wildlife Management Area to the east. These three areas are separated only by highways. State 77 separates Tonawanda and

Iroquois, and Knowlesville Road separates Oak Orchard and Iroquois.

This once-extensive marshland, descended from a glacial lake, was endangered by the drainage programs of farmers and developers until the U.S. Fish and Wildlife Service acquired the wetland in 1985 to establish a refuge. The water level and flow are controlled by dikes, drainage channels, and ditches. Shallow paddies are planted with buckwheat and millet to provide browsing for the migrant birds.

The federal refuge is named after the Iroquois Confederacy, and the names of the original five Indian nations have been given to the marsh pools — Cayuga Pool, Seneca Pool, Onondaga Pool, Oneida Pool, and Mohawk Pool. The Seneca once lived in this area.

The Iroquois Refuge also supports a resident population of waterfowl during the summer months. During the spring and fall migrations, the waterfowl population explodes, with 40,000 to 80,000 geese arriving during March and April and 7,000 to 8,000 geese arriving in September and October. Several thousand migrating ducks appear with the geese in the spring and fall.

While spring attracts the most birds, it also attracts the biggest crowds, and this can put stress on the birds. During the spring migration, nesting, and brood season from March 1 through July 15, public access is restricted in some areas of the refuge. Spring is a critical time of year for wildlife, particularly after a hard winter. Providing a safe, undisturbed area for migrating birds and other wildlife is the primary mission of the refuge.

There are various hiking routes to the marsh pools. The longest trail follows Feeder Road and runs for three miles from Lewiston Road in the south across the entire width of the refuge to West Shelby Road in the north. This trail takes you past four of the pools. Farther east, a mile-long trail takes you past Onondaga

Pool. The Kanyoo Trail is a short nature trail that makes an easy walk. During the restricted season, areas that remain open for wildlife observation and hiking are Onondaga and Kanyoo Nature Trails and four overlooks.

The Onondaga Trail can be reached via State 77 or State 63. In a round-trip of only two miles, it allows hikers to see a mixed habitat of wetland and forestland, along with hundreds of waterfowl on the Onondaga Pool. A sign at the beginning of the trail shows a Nordic skier, indicating that the trail is also open in winter for cross-country skiing.

After just a short walk, you'll be at the northwestern edge of the Onondaga Pool. During the summer there are often herons in the pool. On the day we were there, we saw scores of ducks. At the 0.3-mile mark, you will enter a forest with trees that arch over the trail. During the summer, ferns line the path. Along the trail are benches erected by members of the Youth Conservation Corps for the benefit of bird-watchers or anyone who wants to rest and enjoy the sights and sounds of the forest. When you come to the third bench, you will have reached the end of the trail. From there it's about a twenty-minute walk back to your car.

The forest provides homes for more than thirty mammal species, including white-tailed deer, opossum, mink, red and gray fox, squirrel, and rabbit. Muskrats and beavers live in the wetland area. More than 200 species of birds have been identified in the refuge. Bald eagles have been reintroduced to the area and have adapted well.

The Iroquois headquarters provides information on regional wildlife protection areas, exhibits, interpretative walks on its own trails, and films in the auditorium. There's also information on the Tonawanda and Oak Orchard Wildlife Management Areas.

Where: You can reach State 77 from the west or east via the New York Thruway. Take exit 48A and drive north on State 77 for five miles to the intersection with State 63. Follow State 77 north for the next 1.5 miles to the village of Alabama. The Iroquois National Wildlife Refuge headquarters is one mile north of the village on Casey Road.

Hours: Sunrise to sunset, year-round.

Admission: Free.

Best time to visit: For large flocks of migrating birds, March, April, September, October.

Activities: Cross-country skiing, bird-watching, wildlife observation, nature walks.

Pets: Not allowed.

For more information:

Iroquois National Wildlife Refuge, PO Box 517, Casey Road, Alabama, NY 14003; 716-948-5445.

REINSTEIN WOODS

I arrived early for the guided nature walk and was rewarded by the sight of two young fawns prancing in the parking lot. I was to learn that it pays to be ahead of the crowd at the Dr. Victor Reinstein Woods Nature Preserve, a unique sanctuary in the heart of the heavily developed Buffalo suburb of Cheektowaga.

Just eight miles from downtown Buffalo, the 275-acre preserve has been called a unique biological museum that shows what western New York was like before the first Europeans arrived in the seventeenth and eighteenth centuries. Within the preserve are sixty-five acres of primeval forest that existed before the European settlement of the area in the 1820s.

The southern third of the preserve was part of the old Buffalo Creek Indian Reservation, granted to the Iroquois after the Revolutionary War. The reservation was gradually sold off by the Native Americans between 1842 and 1846. The northern two-thirds of the preserve was owned by early settlers of Cheektowaga,

It's not uncommon for a doe to have twins

who purchased long, narrow land parcels from the Holland Land
Company. By a stroke of good fortune, the Holland Land Company's survey ran a boundary along of the edge of the ancient
forest. Thus these backlot buffer zones were among the few areas
that remained uncut by the newcomers.

The woods would surely have been cut in the post-World
War II rush for development of Cheektowaga if the lands had not
been purchased by Victor Reinstein in 1932. A physician, attorney, and land developer, Reinstein was also fascinated by en-
gineering; he designed and built nineteen ponds on his lands. He
also planted thousands of trees and built roads and a stone house,
which is now sealed. He loved his lands and worked throughout
his life to preserve and enhance them.

After his death and several years of negotiations between
his family and the state, the Department of Environmental
Conservation assumed ownership of and responsibility for the
preserve in 1986.

A beautiful, fragile place, the preserve is a special treasure considering the proximity of heavy development outside its boundaries. The mission here is to protect, preserve, perpetuate, and enhance the area's natural resources. To fulfill this mission, access to the preserve is by guided nature walk only. This is an obvious benefit to the wildlife. However, it can be a detriment to nature lovers, because chances of seeing wildlife are best if humans arrive quietly and in very small numbers. I solved the problem by walking ahead of the group.

It was a hot, sunny day, but we were immediately enveloped in deep shade. Old-growth beech, maple, and black-cherry trees are more than 100 feet high and block most of the sunlight. This is nature's cathedral, and, as in the marble and stone cathedrals of Europe, there is a feeling of reverence here. It seemed as if we were walking on hallowed ground.

There were surprises around every bend. We came to a clearing, and a great blue heron majestically soared overhead. In front of us was a charming sight—a pond, probably more than five acres, completely covered in water lilies with bright pink flowers. Except for the few patches of open water, it didn't even look like a pond, but more like a field of flowers. The lilies were planted by Victor Reinstein's wife, Julia.

At one end of the pond we saw a beaver lodge, and standing on the lodge were—not beavers, but a pair of fawns. As the rest of the group came up, the deer bolted into the woods and to the sanctuary area. The sanctuary area is totally off-limits to visitors and is visited only by the preserve's resident naturalist.

Later we saw a pair of does in the woods and a buck and a doe across the lake. Virtually all species of wildlife native to the area, including white-tailed deer, beaver, waterfowl, red-tailed hawk, pileated woodpecker, and the majestic great blue heron, live in or visit the woods and thrive within its protection.

As we circled the lake, I stopped and looked at a pond on the other side of the path. Suddenly there was a loud rustle in the underbrush, and a large buck bounded away. He had been bedded down in the brush just about ten feet from where I was standing. On the return to the parking lot another deer ran across the road just in front of a young boy and me. Five minutes later I was driving down a major expressway.

Where: Entrance to the preserve is 100 yards south of Como Park Boulevard on Honorine Drive (Honorine was Dr. Reinstein's first wife). Take the New York Thruway to exit 49. Take Transit South to Como Park Boulevard. Go west on Como Park.
Hours: From May 1 to August 31, public nature walks are held the last three Saturdays of every month at 9:00 A.M. and 1:00 P.M. and every Wednesday at 9:00 A.M. and 1:00 P.M. From September 1 through April 30, walks are offered only at 9:00 A.M. Visitors are allowed only as part of the guided nature walk. Groups and organizations can arrange tours at other times.
Admission: Free.
Best time to visit: Birds are most plentiful in spring and fall. Be sure to bring mosquito repellent during the summer months.
Activities: Guided nature walks.
Pets: Not allowed.
Other: Visitors must remain on the trails. There is no camping, picnicking, bicycling, cross-country skiing, or jogging.
For more information:
    Dr. Victor Reinstein Woods Nature Preserve, 77 Honorine Drive, Depew, NY 14043; 716-683-5959.

BEAVER ISLAND STATE PARK

People first camped on the lands now occupied by Grand Island's Beaver Island State Park 3,500 years ago. Grand Island, the Niagara River's largest island, was called Oewanungah by the Neuter Indians, Ga-We-Not by the Senecas who conquered them, and La Grande Isle by the French explorers.

    The great oak forests of Grand Island brought commercialization, and the sawmill town of Whitehaven became a center for wood for barrel staves. In 1833 the East Boston Company of Massachusetts bought 16,000 acres of woodland and stripped the island of its oak forests for use in building clipper ships. By the mid-1800s lumbering had given way to expansive cattle ranches, grand hotels, and magnificent homes.

Remnants of a bygone era make up today's 952-acre Beaver Island State Park on the southern tip of the island. One of the most imposing structures in the park is River Lea, home of cattle rancher and farmer Lewis F. Allen, uncle of Grover Cleveland, the twenty-second president of the United States. He was the second mayor of nearby Buffalo to become president. Built in 1849, this locally designated historic site is home of the Grand Island Historical Society.

Allen's farm formed the nucleus of land designated in 1935 as Beaver Island State Park. The Civilian Conservation Corps contributed significantly to the early development of the park, including the building of the prominent and very popular Casino and Bathhouse that was destroyed in a spectacular fire in October 1992. Plans are under way to rebuild the casino.

Today, the main attraction of the park during the summer is the half-mile of sandy beach, which is clean and well maintained. Though the Niagara River is famous for its currents, the waters off the beach are safe for swimming, and lifeguards are on duty. The upper Niagara River offers sports enthusiasts great fishing just offshore. There's an eighty-slip, sheltered marina, and the park is a popular weekend destination for boaters. Port calls of up to two weeks are possible.

The sight of great blue herons stalking dinner at the edge of the lagoon and the distinctive honk of Canada geese coming in for a landing are familiar happenings in the park. A visit to the Nature Center or a walk along one of the nature trails offers the opportunity to learn about the creatures that inhabit the park.

During the winter months, the park is open for cross-country skiing and snowshoeing. The sledding hill is popular with the younger set and families. Snowmobiling across the frozen landscape and ice fishing along the shore are other favorite cold-weather activities.

There's a USGA-recognized, championship eighteen-hole course in the park. The popular 6,779-yard, par-72 course offers wide, tree-lined fairways. The park also has nine picnic shelters (some with electricity), playgrounds, a soccer field, baseball, basketball, volleyball, and horseshoes. There's a boardwalk along the beach and changing facilities. The Nature Center, operated by the Schoellkopf Geological Museum in Niagara Falls, offers programs and guided nature walks in the park.

Where: Grand Island is about 15 minutes north of Buffalo. Take the New York Thruway north and then the Beaver Island exit.
Hours: Dawn to dusk. The park is open year-round, but most buildings are open only in the summer.
Admission: $4.00 per vehicle from the end of June through Labor Day; free otherwise.
Best time to visit: The park tends to be quite crowded on sunny summer weekends. Try to visit during the week, if possible. During the spring and fall the park attracts a number of migrating birds. Winter can be starkly beautiful along the Niagara River, whether you are skiing or just enjoying a walk along the river.
Activities: Swimming, boating, nature walks, skiing, snowshoeing, snowmobiling, golf, fishing.
Concessions: Snack bar and marina.
Pets: Must be under control at all times. Dogs must be restrained by a leash not exceeding six feet and are not allowed in designated bathing areas.
For more information:
Beaver Island State Park, Grand Island, NY 14072; 716-773-3271.

EVANGOLA STATE PARK

The big attraction at Evangola State Park on the shores of Lake

Erie is the beautiful arc-shaped shoreline—a long, clean, sandy beach that is perfect for swimming and beachcombing. It is one of the finest swimming areas on the Niagara Frontier. Just inland from the lake, campers can choose from among eighty sites.

The park, which is twenty-five miles southwest of Buffalo, opened in 1954 on former farmlands that used to grow tomatoes, beans, and corn. A variety of habitats exist here, including lakeshore, woodland, meadow, and wetlands. Wildlife in the park includes white-tailed deer, raccoons, turkeys, and redtail hawks. Scattered over the land are stones brought in across the lake from Canada during the last Ice Age. These stones are often speckled black and white or striped.

There are facilities for baseball, soccer, tennis, volleyball, horseshoes, and basketball. Limited sports equipment may be borrowed from the bathhouse. Picnic tables overlook the lake, and a number are accessible to people with limited mobility. Seven picnic shelters accommodating fifty to sixty people each are available. There's lifeguard protection at the beach. The campground has flush toilets and hot showers. Electric and handicapped-accessible sites are available.

Where: Take State 5 south from Buffalo to Evangola State Park Road, near Farnham.

Hours: The park is open from dawn to dusk year-round; the campground is open from mid-April to mid-October.

Admission: $4.00 per car during the summer season; free the rest of the year. Campsites are $10.00 to $13.50.

Best time to visit: Weekends during the summer are the most popular. June and September can be warm and delightful.

Concessions: Snack bar.

Activities: Field sports, tennis, basketball, horseshoes, picnicking, swimming, camping, beachcombing, wildlife observation.

Pets: Dogs are not allowed in designated bathing areas and must be restrained by a leash not exceeding six feet in other areas.

For more information:

Evangola State Park, Irving, NY 14081; 716-549-1802.
Campsite reservations, 800-456-CAMP.

Index

Titles in the Natural Wonders/Green Guide series:

Natural Wonders of Alaska
Natural Wonders of Connecticut & Rhode Island
Natural Wonders of Florida
Green Guide to Hawaii
Natural Wonders of Idaho
Natural Wonders of Massachusetts
Natural Wonders of Michigan
Natural Wonders of New Hampshire
Natural Wonders of New Jersey
Natural Wonders of New York
Natural Wonders of Ohio
Green Guide to Oregon
Natural Wonders of Southern California
Natural Wonders of Texas
Natural Wonders of Vermont
Natural Wonders of Virginia
Green Guide to Washington
Natural Wonders of Wisconsin

All books are $9.95 at bookstores.
Or order directly from the publisher (add $3.00 shipping and
handling for direct orders):

Country Roads Press
P.O. Box 286
Castine, Maine 04421
Toll-free phone number: **800-729-9179**